A Sense for the Other

The Timeliness and Relevance of Anthropology

Marc Augé

Translated by Amy Jacobs

Stanford University Press
Stanford, California

A Sense for the Other: The Timeliness and Relevance of Anthropology was originally published in French in 1994 under the title *Le Sens des autres: Actualité de l'anthropologie*, © 1994 by Librairie Arthème Fayard. The Preface has been prepared especially for this edition by Marc Augé.

Assistance for the translation was provided by the French Ministry of Culture.

Stanford University Press
Stanford, California

© 1998 by the Board of Trustees of the Leland Stanford Junior University
Printed in the United States of America

CIP data appear at the end of the book

Acknowledgments

My particular thanks to Michel Aghassian, whose help in preparing the manuscript was precious, and to my loyal collaborators, Christine Cailletau and Stéphane Vaillant.

M.A.

Contents

Preface to the English Edition

This brief preface is meant to enable the English-speaking reader to situate the present book within my personal itinerary as an anthropologist as well as in the broader context of anthropological research.

Each of us has a particular itinerary and each of us has been influenced in his or her intellectual development by particular thinkers. During my stay in Ivory Coast, which stretched roughly from 1965 to 1970, and later, when I was conducting research in Togo, I considered myself—and still do consider myself—to be working in the current of thought developed by Max Gluckman in England and, somewhat later, Georges Balandier in France. A number of Africanists of my generation followed these thinkers in believing that historical knowledge was the necessary prerequisite to all anthropological study. History affected and to a certain degree explained the facts we had before our eyes. And we were conscious—how could it have been otherwise in that period of profound transformation following decolonization?—that we were far from being finished with history: it was in action right before our eyes, and in a way, we were part of it.

Understanding this did not mean, however (as it did for some of my colleagues), that I found uninteresting, without purpose, or irrelevant work which, in a different spirit, privileged the study of the structural relations that close attention to myths, kinship, and representations of personhood can bring to light. The dominant theme of this research was not that these sectors didn't change but that they were transformed–that from a formal perspective, the way they changed was not at all arbitrary. It was not inconceivable to me that we could attend simultaneously to the strong forces of change operating in Africa at the time *and* to structural phenomena, which enable us to perceive more clearly the logic or contradictions of such change.

What we were seeing of history in the making invited us to take as valid anthropological objects phenomena that others might have judged less "pure" or "significant" than systems of filiation or matrimonial alliance, for example. This sense of the importance of history explains why I was particularly sensitive to the spectacle that the lagoon societies of Ivory Coast set before my eyes. I'm referring to the ensemble of social interactions to which events such as illness and death gave rise–the scenarios of accusation, counteraccusation, or negotiation expressed in the language of witchcraft–and the prophetic movements, surprisingly long-lived, that had appeared at the beginning of the century. Since the prophet Harris made his appearance in 1913-14, Ivorian prophet-healers had been struggling both to cure individuals and to deliver a message about the meaning of their situation. The history of these prophets, which may be identified in part with the development of the Harris church, was a long one. Some of those who had gotten their start in the 1930s were still in place in 1970, and new prophets were gathering followers. Today, ever more numerous, the prophets continue to treat individuals and to judge–sometimes approvingly, often critically–the policies of the state (political independence in no way meant that they had no more to say on this subject).

I studied various forms of the ritual activity by which the prophets sought to manage the relations of otherness that are inscribed in the logic of lineage-based systems, notably in the matter of witchcraft accusations. I was also interested in new figures of otherness, not merely the relations between colonizers and colonized but those between economic developers and their "developees," between rich and poor, bosses and employees, politicians and ordinary citizens, and so forth. However attuned to the moment and (in a sense) mod-

ern the prophets' activity was, it nonetheless remained, in the forms
specific to it, essentially ritualistic. I was therefore not disoriented
when, a short time later, in Togo, I began studying more "classical"
and ancient ritual forms, forms that we know to be the mold for the
so-called syncretic religions of South America and the Antilles.

My general reflection on ritual and otherness has this African experience as its source and inspiration. I tried, in effect, to pinpoint
and analyze within African societies formal invariances that were
practices, namely, ritualized practices, rather than rule systems or
preconstituted narratives. Thus defined, my object obliged me to
take into account the power relations among the actors–which was
something that witchcraft scenarios and the personal history of each
prophet, whether one of relative success or total failure, invited me
to do. Africa, it seemed to me, demonstrated the artificiality of certain theoretical oppositions.

But from the moment the opposition between dynamic and structural approaches was relativized, another opposition was called into
question. Why trace a line of demarcation between societies believed to warrant or require anthropological observation and others
(namely, our own) thought to demand a different type of study?
Once anthropology, through its study of rites, takes social meaning–that is, the intellectual and institutional procedures through
which human beings render their reciprocal relations thinkable and
possible–as its principal object, the necessity for a generalized anthropology, one that includes the whole planet, seems obvious. All
the more so given that the current acceleration of history, together
with developments in circulation, in information gathering and dissemination, and the type of communication indissociable from
them, affect simultaneously, albeit unequally, all corners of the
earth. In short, if anthropology is not possible everywhere, it is not
possible anywhere. At the same time, the issues of otherness and ritual have never been more relevant. To put it simply, I believe anthropology has a future.

The object of all ritual activity is ultimately, it seems to me, to
constitute a relation. The otherness which that relation relativizes
may be individual (that of a friend of the same age group, a relative,
or a personal ally, for example) or collective (concerning people's
membership in different groups). Whether individual or collective,

identity is in all cases relative. It is always constructed through ne-gotiation with an otherness that is itself relative, and it is this nego-tiation that becomes the object of ritual activity. With this in mind, we may conclude that here and now, today and in its very places of origin–Europe, the United States–there has in fact been no change in the intellectual object of anthropology, even though the death of exoticism, the end of the "great divide" between the West and the "others," and generalized globalization have modified both the stakes involved and the conditions of anthropology's practice. The question is, how do we ask–and answer–the question of otherness, and consequently that of anthropology's role, in a world marked by the triple excess–excess information, excess images, and excessive recourse to the idea or value of "the individual"–that I propose to call "supermodernity" (*surmodernité*)?

An Introductory Word

My title–*A Sense for the Other* (*Le Sens des autres*)– may be understood in two ways. First, having a sense for the other, like having a sense of family, direction, or rhythm, might be considered an innate (or acquired) gift of the sort that varies from individual to individual, group to group, period to period. In Europe today the sense for the other, for otherness, is both being lost and becoming more acute. It is being lost in the sense that the aptitude for tolerating otherness–difference–is disappearing. And yet that very intolerance itself creates, invents, and structures otherness. Nationalism, regionalism, fundamentalism, systematic attempts at "ethnic cleansing"–all involve less a crisis of identity than a kind of uncontrolled heating up of the processes that generate otherness. As though searching for a relevant level of collective identity (an identity that they unduly substantialize), certain human groups keep secreting otherness. And in thus fabricating "others" they themselves decompose, as if, in direct contrast to the process of cellular differentiation, such incessant social differentiation resulted in death.

In its second meaning, *le sens des autres* refers to "the sense *of* the other"; that is, the others' "sense" or that which has meaning for others. Here the other is no longer object but subject, the generator of meaning: we are confronted with the sense that others, whether individuals or social groups, elaborate for themselves. But the two meanings go hand in hand, for in both cases the "sense" in question is social meaning, the constellation of symbolic relations instituted among and lived by people within a given social group, such that the group can in fact be identified as such by that constellation of relations. Anthropology is first and foremost the anthropological study of the others' anthropology. This is because no society exists that has not defined, more or less strictly, a series of "normal"–that is, instituted and symbolic–relations between generations, first-born children and their siblings, men and women, allies, lineages, age groups, free persons and captives, indigenous members and foreigners, and so on. An anthropologist's first task is to draw the map of this relative identity and otherness.

As we have discovered, such an undertaking need not concern exclusively one type of society. In the present work, in which my frame of reference as an Africanist and my more global preoccupations overlap, I have sought, in positing the premises of a "generalized" anthropology, to explore the concept of otherness in its double relativity–for, as we know, others also define what is for them "the other." This exploration leads to a further question. Given that our particular present is characterized by the death of exoticism, we may legitimately wonder under what conditions anthropology without exoticism is possible and to what ends it should be practiced. To shed some light on the answer, I will occasionally evoke my personal professional itinerary in this book, a volume that combines articles published separately over the last decade with new material in what I hope will prove a useful way. The primary interest of that itinerary is that it has confronted me with diverse types of otherness. Over the years I have tried to understand what these diverse types might have in common.

A Sense for the Other

*The Timeliness
and Relevance of
Anthropology*

1 Who Is the Other?

To retrace and reexamine an itinerary that, after taking me from Paris to Africa, then brought me back to France without my feeling that I had given up my distant points of reference—this may seem to involve retrospectively creating a coherence that we know to be illusory. But it is also an occasion for asking more fundamental questions. What is the researcher searching for? And if it's the other, who is the other?

The social sciences have been trying for several years to define methods (more specifically, methods based on a redefinition of the object) that will allow them to escape overly abstract interpretive models without succumbing to the easy solutions made available by historicism or cultural relativism. The issue of the social sciences' scientificity and that of their models of interpretation may be seen as tied to the question of the other. Our immersion in the world we study condemns us to practice a pragmatic anthropology, to use Kant's expression, and in ethnology the whole question is whether the supposed exteriority of our object is so assured as to free us from this particular constraint. Such exteriority is problematic. It is defined by three parameters which must be kept distinct and yet not be allowed to become mutually exclusive. First, there is the scientificity or paradigm requirement, which enables us to master the instability of the social object. Second, there is our recognition of a kind of cultural, social, historical, and psychological otherness that corresponds to a real difference between the observer and what he or she observes, be it a group or an individual. And finally there is the opposite recognition, the counter-reality; namely, that the observer is situated inside the object, if only in the sense that for him or her no less than for Terence, nothing that is human is unknown. Every anthropologist's itinerary may be measured against these parameters, and it is useful to have numerous testimonies at our disposal. I belong to the ethnological condition just as Montaigne belonged to the human condition, a belonging that he understood as allowing him to suppose that his particular account and testimony would be of interest to other representatives of the same condition.

To speak of itineraries is to speak of departure, sojourning, and return, although it should be understood that there were several departures, that sojourning was also traveling, and that the return has never been definitive.

At the start there is the cultural other—the one who piques the curiosity and concern of lay people, in some instances members of the ethnologist's own family, who question him or her about the exact nature of the craft: "So, you live with various tribes, you study their ways of life?" Coming perhaps readily to the tongue of meagerly informed interlocutors, this last expression, "ways of life," is interesting in that, while it refers to instituted usages, it seems to evoke natural ones, by which I mean it inscribes social practice within nature, even as the word "custom" can give such practice something like a historical foundation. Whether or not it is apprehended in terms of an evolutionist vision of society, the others' culture is spontaneously defined as a sort of nature—a rather particular one, however: an instituted nature, one that can be described in juridical terms, for example (which is precisely what French colonial administrators set out to do in their *coutumiers*).[1] To describe this spontaneous point of view we might have recourse to a fairly common expression more readily applied to individuals than groups: "second nature." The culture of others is imagined as a second nature to them.

When leaving in 1965 for the lagoons of southern Ivory Coast, I was not much more knowledgeable than a layman, but I was keenly conscious that I was going to study other *cultures*. The literature about the term "culture" was already prolific and showed no signs of running dry; it is not my purpose here to take an inventory of it. Suffice it to say that in France in the 1960s, the debate about culture took a new turn and has remained unresolved ever since, though at this retrospective distance we have a clearer vision of the issues involved.

In the 1960s what was being called into question was the functionalist vision of society, and with it the functionalist vision of culture. I use the term here to refer to both the strictly cultural-functionalist point of view, according to which the convergence of cultural "traits" has meaning within a singular configuration to which it gives both style and coherence, and the Marxist point of view, according to which culture as an ensemble of values may be deduced from the economic infrastructure–a definition hardly exclusive to Marxists. What was being questioned at the time was the belief in final causes that inspired the first point of view and the mechanistic presuppositions that inspired the second.

The debate has several origins and has been fueled by several authors; let me just point out in this connection a rather remarkable convergence. *Sociologie et anthropologie*, a collection of texts by Marcel Mauss with a prefatory essay by Claude Lévi-Strauss, came out first in 1950 but a third, expanded edition was released in 1966.[2] Cornelius Castoriadis's *L'Institution imaginaire de la société*, which appeared in 1975, includes a number of articles that had originally been published in *Socialisme ou Barbarie* between 1964 and 1965.[3] And Louis Althusser's *Pour Marx* was published in 1965.[4]

Lévi-Strauss's essay, *Introduction to the Work of Marcel Mauss*, is a rich text that possibly allows for contradictory interpretations. I have retained those that seem to me to have been at the source of the antifunctionalist movement. Lévi-Strauss wrote that symbolism precedes knowledge: language "can only have arisen all at once" (p. 59), and with the advent of language the universe came to signify, but it was not as a result any better understood. At the origin, then, there was a "signifier-totality" that man was "at a loss to know how to allocate to a signified, given as such, but no less unknown for being given" (p. 62). In his effort to understand the world, which he comes to know only little by little, man thus has at his permanent disposal a "surplus of signification" that he "shares out among things in accordance with the laws of the symbolic thinking which it is the task of ethnologists and linguists to study" (pp. 62–63). Clearly the laws by which symbolism establishes relations are, for Lévi-Strauss, intrinsic to man: they precede his acting on the world, for they are the instrument of such action rather than the product of it. If we keep to his analysis, we can say that the material origin of symbolism is to be found in the human brain, not in the economic infrastructure, which on the contrary presupposes the existence of symbolism.

The priority of symbolism has another effect. If culture is to be defined as an ensemble of symbolic systems at the forefront of which stand "language, the matrimonial rules, the economic relations, art, science, and religion" (p. 16), then the individual's condition is defined by a necessary alienation. Referring explicitly to an article by Jacques Lacan published in 1948,[5] Lévi-Strauss remarks: "Strictly speaking, the person whom we call sane is the one who is capable of alienating himself, since he consents to an existence in a world definable only by the self-other relationship" (p. 108). It is only in and through social life, the actualization of self's relation to others, that a symbolic structure can be developed that is equally available to all members of society. But at the same time, social life for each person involves putting into operation and combining systems that define such life and exist prior to any concrete relation.

Castoriadis seems to have been thinking along lines consistent with Lévi-Strauss's definitions when he wrote that ways of organizing the economy, systems of law, power structures, and religions "exist socially as sanctioned symbolic systems."[6] Quite logically, Castoriadis used the same term, "alienation," to describe the individual's relation to institutions and social life in general. He deliberately assumed an antifunctionalist and antimechanistic stance by affirming that institutions cannot be reduced to their economic or functional components: there is never, in his view, a pure relation of exteriority between an institution and those who use it or who are in some way affected by it or concerned with it. Distinguishing between the questions of alienation and class division, Castoriadis pointed out that alienation exists even in societies that are not structured into social classes. It is this insight that enables us to perceive a striking kinship between his analyses and Althusser's. When Castoriadis writes that in a class society, the dominant class itself is in a state of alienation and that "it cannot mystify the rest of society with its ideology without at the same time mystifying itself," he is very close to the theses on class ideology in particular–and ideology in general–of *For Marx*.

This detour through *l'air du temps* of the 1960s is not without its purpose. First, it was precisely that air that ethnologists of my generation were breathing when we did our first fieldwork. Second, the antifunctionalist critique, while it characterizes in a general way the intellectual atmosphere of the period, was not without its ambiguities, and this made it potentially dangerous for ethnologists, whose role it ran the risk of overestimating, and for ethnology as a whole, whose object it was perhaps distorting. In short, the antifunctionalist critique threatened to replace the "final causes" view of culture with the obscurantist theme of culture-as-mystery. And the danger was all that much greater in that, paradoxically, the experience of culture as second nature was becoming more familiar to us every day. If as ethnologists we had the feeling that by leaving to work abroad we were succumbing to the lure of exotic places, we have no doubt come back wiser: not disappointed exactly, but keenly aware that very soon after one decides to make the effort to bend oneself to unknown rhythms, preoccupations, and priorities, what one actually perceives more clearly each day is the constructed, logical, even familiar character of such rhythms, preoccupations, and priorities. Evans-Pritchard recounts how he surprised himself in the process of formulating interpretations as an Azande would; I have found myself thinking like an Alladian among Alladians, finding natural, for example, the particular logic of witchcraft accusations. Had we for all that toppled over into another world? Were we not in fact rediscovering, behind the specificities of another language, the cruelties, anxieties, and jealousies of any relatively closed social milieu–what I would call the Romorantin effect?[7]

Theoretical thinking on this point was none too clear at the time–or rather, it was both clear and obscure, and there were reasons for the chiaroscuro. When we experience culture as natural and necessary, we can formulate two distinct questions. First, we may wonder how it happens that the particular business of a human individual is to assume the shape of a culture that seems at once the limit and the condition of his or her singular existence. Then we may ask what accounts for the specificity of a particular culture, given that all those who belong to that culture in some way bear its mark, whatever their respective places or roles in the society.

The two questions are distinguishable from each other; I insist on this all the more firmly because the distinction is not always made. But it is also true that they partially overlap: the alienation that enables one to fit into the social can only be apprehended within a given cultural configuration. It does not follow from this, however, that the ineffable singularity of each culture, its ultimate specificity, is the secret of alienation, always different, yet always the same. This tacit culturalist temptation may nonetheless be found in the works of several authors, especially during the sixties. It is an ever-present temptation that appears quite clearly in Castoriadis's analyses. His initial move was to expose the symbolic character of every social institution while asking about the "why" of alienation. But by resorting to the notion of *l'imaginaire social*, Castoriadis transformed his original question into why it is that a society needs to look for "the complement necessary to its order" in the imaginary, in its imagination. At the core of that imagination and its imaginings, he spied "something that cannot be reduced to the functional, an original investment by society of the world and itself with meaning—meanings which are not 'dictated' by real factors since it is instead this meaning that attributes to these real factors a particular importance and a particular place in the universe constituted by a given society."[8] In this way the symbolism constraint, the problem of the signifier's necessarily excess meaning, was dissimulated behind imagined, imaginary identity: what Hegel called "the spirit of a people." And from that moment forward it was as though ethnologists were only concerned by a problem of translation, though indeed a formidable one: they must "try to understand the universe of the Babylonians or the Bororos, both their natural and social world, as they lived it, and, in attempting to explain it, to refrain from introducing into it determinations that did not exist for this culture (consciously or unconsciously)."[9] Culture, in this view, is what supplements social existence, what supplements the functional or predetermined universe. As such it may well explain why Bororos are not Babylonians, but not why one cannot *not* be Bororo when one is Bororo nor what it is to be Bororo, Florentine, San Franciscan, or Parisian.

Culture as surplus or supplement–an "extra," we might say–is what is invoked when the functionalist or determinist explanation has been exhausted. The idea of culture as what's left over is opposed to the culture-as-sum-total of the cultural-functionalist definition. To make ethnologists into specialists of culture so defined was obviously both to limit their object, reducing it to what is ineffable–style and specificity–and to expand their role too far, for they were now being assigned the task of explaining the inexplicable and the irreducible. In "Culture et idéologie," an article published in 1966 in the *Cahiers marxistes-léninistes*, Roger Establet tried to define the cultural field by distinguishing, as Pierre Bourdieu had done, between society and culture, between *rapports de force* (power relations) and *rapports de sens* (meaning relations), starting from the fact that not all observed behaviors come down to the use of practices determined by "social" requirements. The example of conspicuous consumption, which ethnologists had recently brought to light, seemed to him sufficient evidence that a behavioral norm could escape strictly social determination. Speaking of culture as an individual acquisition, Edouard Herriot is reported to have said that it is what a man has left when he's forgotten everything else. Culture in the postfunctionalist sense of the term is understood as what a society is left with after it's been completely explained. Economic development technicians and consultants in the third world have often adopted this view of culture, which is in a way akin to what they call "the human factor." It's interesting to note how in 1967 an author like Samir Amin turned to ethnologists to explain why, under conditions fairly comparable to those of their neighbors, the Senufo grew more abundant crops, and why the Lobi and the Kulango had remained outside all movements of modernization.[10]

Had we, then, set out for different cultures in order to discover the secret of their difference and explain what economics and sociology could not? Were we forever condemned to have the last word, specialists of the "wild flowers" of ideology, the supplement of soul, the others' irreducible otherness?

If this was indeed the illusion we left under, we had to give it up fast, for what the ethnologist immediately discovers is not cultures, but societies: hierarchically organized ensembles within which the notions of difference and otherness are already full of meaning. One is fairly quickly made to feel that anyone who wants to do anthropology must first confront the others' anthropology. At first, all he can perceive of it is its instituted form, the one that we can give an account of in juridical or political terms. What he perceives first and foremost are *social* differences.

The lagoon societies I lived in starting in 1965 were not states, but their lineage-based organization gave rise to a multitude of different social statuses and situations. Differences in gender, age, filiation, and lineage; differences in origin (free or servitorial) and generation, all combined to institute a multitude of status positions and codified interrelations. The opposition man/woman, for example, had concrete reality only from the moment that a combination of other determinations was taken into account. The free wife of a lineage chief; the free, captive, or foreign wife of a man disadvantageously situated in the lineage hierarchy; a woman descended from a captive woman (first, second, or third generation); and the captive wife of a captive man had perhaps many things in common—habits, ways of being and living—but the differences between them are much more significant. A postmenopausal woman belonging to the main line of an important lineage was almost the equal of a man and could serve as lineage head, at least temporarily, whereas the fate of a young captive woman depended entirely on the good will of the man who acquired her. When we speak of the status of difference and otherness in a given society, we have to acknowledge that that status cannot be formulated uniformly, that it is not uttered or named (if indeed it is named) or lived in the same way at both ends of the status spectrum.

All of this becomes clear as soon as we find ourselves looking at societies that, as differently organized as they may be from those we know more immediately, are hardly egalitarian or homogeneous. But this is not all. Accepting for the moment a dichotomy that we may be led to question later, I would go so far as to say that social concerns and realities transcend cultural ones, even when what is cultural is conceived of in substantivist terms. I am thinking namely of the language and practice of witchcraft; the suspicions, accusations, confessions, and sanctions that, taken together, are the forms that constitute and express the referent "witchcraft."

In southern Ivory Coast (to take one of many possible examples)

populations exist side by side that could be considered ethno-cultural units in that, despite their common characteristics, they are
more different than similar, be it in the matter of language, lineage
type (some are predominantly patrilinear, others predominantly matrilinear, while all manner of combinations and compromises between these two extremes have been attested), generational organization, age group divisions, or in terms of some other criterion.
Some of the groups in the area where I lived were composed of no
more than ten thousand individuals, a fact that justifies the designation "lagoon mosaic" sometimes applied to the region. Still, this
apparent cultural arbitrariness is conceived of as essentially natural,
or, if one prefers, substantive. Witchcraft power is represented as
attaching to psychic elements which themselves have material existence, discernible in the blood or the shadow cast by a human body.
The effects of this power are likewise material, measurable in terms
of skin pallor, the supposed victim's relative weakness and the fre-
quency of his or her faints and hemorrhages–all manifestations that
can precede, announce, and/or bring on death. Local informers answer the ethnologist's questions willingly, and their answers suggest
categories by means of which we may distinguish between these
ethno-cultural groups, for while witchcraft power is the same in all
of them in that it is never exercised arbitrarily but is instead, in all
cases, assigned an area in which it may be active together with limits
on that activity, these limits are never the same from one group to
another. We may say, for example–although this simplifies the matter–that witchcraft power is exercised patrilinearly among the patrilinearly organized Dida, more exactly by father on son, while
among the matrilinear Alladian it is exercised within the matrilineage, especially by maternal uncle on uterine nephew.

Given these seemingly fundamental cultural regulations, it is remarkable to observe that changes in social status in fact bring with
them substantive changes in the cultural paradigm. Consider, for
example, the relations between the Alladian, who were seaside mer-
chants, and their female Dida captives. Many Alladian men married
Dida women in exchange for a dowry; the advantage of such a wife in
the eyes of a rich Alladian merchant was that she ensured him an exclusively Alladian descendance. Cut off from the patrilinear society
of the mother, their children would be wholly attached to the matri-

lineage of their Alladian father, whereas a child born of an Alladian mother was necessarily related and could only be considered in reference to two lineages representing two potentially rival principles of authority. Captive men and women and their descendants all offered the same advantage to the Alladian and were integrated smoothly into Alladian lineages, the memory of their origin fading over the generations without ever being completely effaced. But such ethnic and social assimilation entails a change in the cultural paradigm, the effect of a kind of rhetoric or algebra whose casuistic character we might in other contexts admire: My captive is my daughter; I can give her in marriage to another; I can also marry her myself or have children with her; functionally she is my sister, since she belongs to my matrilineage; and even though she is Dida and regardless of who the father of her children is, those children will be with me in a possible, virtual witchcraft relation. We see that no matter how incarnate and substantive the powers of aggression and death are, they change in accordance with the social remodeling resulting, for example, from the systematic practice among wealthy Alladian lineages of taking captives from and allying themselves matrimonially with patrilinear societies.

This is only one example of the treatment of otherness that characterizes the practical and ritual activity of lineage-based societies. It is a game played on the borders, tending either to assimilate the other and thus set off the internal dynamic of difference or to expulse the other in order to mark the limits of identity (all abominable and antinatural practices are attributed to foreigners, who are considered *absolute* others). It is fairly obvious how this way of dividing up the world works in ethnic terms. In terms of gender, it can lead to certain women becoming quasi men, while in terms of status it can make certain captives quasi freemen. Dealing with the other is really an indirect or negative way (perhaps the only one possible) of thinking or conceiving the same, the identical: the *ethnos* or ethnic group, fully realized man, a pure lineage. Ethnology has discerned this phenomenon in the segmentary logic of groups who only identify themselves by distinguishing themselves from others at different levels of solidarity and/or opposition—a vast movement of comprehension and extension that accounts for a significant part of social or political life. But such logic is even more general, I believe, and works deeply upon and within a part of humanity for whom the individual's identity is just as problematic—not, as may be presumed, nonexistent—as group identity.

It can happen that group identity is affirmed under circumstances that we might expect would lead those involved to challenge it. Slave revolts were practically unknown in lineage-based Africa. Moreover, it is willingly admitted that while the power of a strong man is ambivalent, either beneficent or maleficent, it remains in any case legitimate as long as it shows itself to be unflinching and emanates from a social position that implies it. When the suspicion of witchcraft has led to an accusation and the supposed witches are summoned to confess, they admit their crimes in the very same terms that were used to accuse them; it is not possible for them to affirm that they themselves do not adhere to the reasons of their accusers. In this they are like those captive Amazonion warriors, the Tupinamba. Left relatively free in their movements, they were less prisoner to those who vanquished them than to the values they shared with the victors; it was neither possible or thinkable for captive Tupinamba to flee the fatal torment they must one day undergo.[11]

We perceive here a point of resistance, a provocative piece of unthought-through material, a weight, about which it would be very difficult to say whether it is of social or cultural origin. Neither of these two qualifiers really seems relevant once we set about describing actual behaviors. It is as if, by leaning too hard on the distinction between cultural and social, we made it impossible to understand what within a given society acts as efficient cause, what makes things run. It is here that the observer's way of conceptualizing is called into question by that of the observed—for others *think* what their relations are; they too are conceivers of identity and otherness. What we call institutions, social order, filiation, and alliance are inscribed in the others' thinking of and about identity, otherness, and relation—though, as it happens, their thought is not constructed in the same terms as the ethnologist's questions.

I do not mean to say that their thought is inaccessible to those who ask the questions, but that often the questions impose their language and economy on the answers. This perverse effect can be evaluated at two levels in the African example. First, to the extent that the questions try to make manifest a systematic totality–relevant totalities would be, in increasing degree of extension, a "system of beliefs in and about witchcraft," a "religion," a "culture"–they formulate a statement that has no strict equivalent for the ethnologist's interlocutors. No Alladian, Ashanti, or Ewe has ever elaborated or uttered the ensemble of discourses that ethnologists call the Alladian, Ashanti, or Ewe "thought system," "religion," or "philosophy." Such systematic totalities most often result from the ethnologist's putting partial responses, analyses, exegeses, and informants' commentaries, which have been more or less solicited by questions, together with his or her own interpretations, sensitive as he or she is to regularities, convergences, implicit significations, and the virtual logic that underlies the diversity of observed facts and obtained answers. Even in the best of circumstances, when an ethnographical study is carefully conducted and inferences are made rigorously, the discursive status of the whole thus constituted has no equivalent in the observable practices whose latent coherence the ethnologist has worked to make explicit. Ethnologists probably cannot proceed in any other way, and to the extent that we remain conscious of what we are doing, such work serves a valuable heuristic function. But it also tends to harden, homogenize, almost to reify the others' otherness. The Benin philosopher Paulin Hountondji criticized the Reverend Father Tempels and his *Philosophie bantoue* for what he considered an extreme form of this tendency, calling it "ethnophilosophy." By this Hountondji meant an imaginative search–giving imaginary results–for a vision of the world that might be assimilated to an immutable collective philosophy.[12] Hountondji astutely criticizes Tempels for assuming that just as French philosophy consists of the ensemble of philosophic works written by French people, so Bantu "philosophy" could somehow be deduced from Bantu practices as if it were consubstantial with the being of Bantu-speaking populations.

In addition to affecting the overall status of spoken words, the ethnologist's questions also influence the meaning of them: the questions themselves affect the meaning that the ethnologist, with or without the help of a translator, gives to the answers. Those of us who wrote monographs in the sixties discovered precious information and, occasionally, quite subtle analyses in the literature written by colonial administrators, officers, and missionaries, but we also encountered an uncertain, perilous vocabulary. Such approximative use of words has also characterized the writings of professional ethnologists, and as far as I know the phenomenon is not exclusive to Africa or Africanists. It is particularly striking in discussions of what, since Marcel Mauss, we have agreed to call the notion of "person." The literature mentions in this connection the plural "soul" that constitutes African or Amerindian individuality (among others). I discovered that the Ashanti have two "souls," the *kra* and the *sunsum*, definitions of which vary according to the author consulted. For some, the *kra* was a guardian, a spiritual being that left a person at the moment of death, while the *sunsum* was a "bird-soul," more or less stable. For others, otherwise influenced, the *kra* was like the id of the Freudian topic while the *sunsum* was the equivalent of the ego.

Whatever the interpretive approximations and a priori judgments of these observers, they should at least be credited with sensing in many cases where the disturbance in the encounter with the other was located. It was not in some mysterious ethno-cultural essence of which each and every singular existence was merely the expression or illustration—The Ashanti are different from the Malinke in the same way as stock flowers are from dahlias—but indeed in the conception, utterly subversive of Western notions, of identity and alterity, especially of the relation between self and others. If the question "Who is the other?" is indeed at the bottom of all anthropological debate, then the "others," those whom the anthropologist chooses to study, must be party to that debate. Having set out to question the others about what made them different, a certain number of ethnologists—a certain number of us—found ourselves being more or less directly questioned about what constituted *our* identity. But this return to sender, a kind of *arroseur arrosé*, was never formulated as such. What happened instead was that every once in a while some lofty informant like Gedegbe, the last diviner of Behanzin and privileged interlocutor of the French colonial administrator and ethnologist Bernard Maupoil, turned out to be quite skillful at reflecting, in the manner of a philosopher and in his own name, on the rites he himself practiced. As I discovered, an ethnologist's questioning arises gradually from the reiterated observation of different ritual stagings on the occasion of births, accidents, illnesses, deaths; from analysis of different symbolic devices and procedures; and from an attentive consideration of local interpretations and exegeses. It is in this way that the ethnologist may move from something obvious–the differences constitutive of social life–to a problem area: the internal multiplicity of the self.

Ethnologists, and even certain of their predecessors, sensed very early on that the pagans of Africa, America, and the South Sea Islands had their own conceptions of self and other. In each case these were expressed in a vocabulary that was for all intents and purposes untranslatable, even when administrators and ethnologists made use, as the best of them did, of gloss and paraphrase. To speak only of Africa, the first thing the lineage-based ritual apparatus stages is a plural self, relational and thereby relative. This was in any case the rediscovery that my African interlocutors soon imposed on me. The conviction they shared, regardless of their different social statuses, a conviction they either expressed in words or conveyed by their behavior, may be summed up as follows: individuals only exist by way of the relations that unite them.

In this sense, the individual is only the necessary and variable intersection of an ensemble of relations. The scenarios called forth by death or illness, the suspicions or accusations of witchcraft that I studied in Ivory Coast, were in this respect quite revealing. The powers they put under accusation and supposedly put into play could hardly be called exclusively spiritual *or* corporeal (the local anthropology is not dualist), and they have reality and meaning only as a function of the social relation, one of whose possibilities they actualize. Among the Alladian or the Ashanti, for example, it is between uterine brothers, or else by maternal uncle on uterine nephew (or in the opposite direction), that witchcraft aggression is practiced. This means that an illness or a death can call certain social relations into question and not others. But it also means that the elements from which a person derives his or her witchcraft power or that make a person vulnerable to its attack–elements that are also constituents of the individual personality–do not define the individual as a self-contained being consubstantial with himself or herself. On the contrary, the individual only exists by way of his or her position in a system of relations whose main parameters are filiation and alliance, a system itself made manifest by these components, which themselves only exist within and through the relation to others of which they are the instrument.

This multileveled representation of what is not merely an individual's psychic organization, but what corresponds in certain aspects to such an organization, is very widespread in Africa. It is also often more complex than what I have just outlined, but I only wish to insist here on its essentially relative and relational character, and to propose a brief analysis of the model attested throughout a vast region of West Africa. First it should be noted that the model has undergone the respective influences of two important kingdoms: the Ashanti kingdom in what is now Ghana and the Yoruba kingdom in what is now Nigeria. I myself moved from one zone of influence to another when working in Togo in the 1970s. At so vast a scale, it is easy to site points of similarity and transmission, word-borrowings, term-permutations, and structural permanencies, but these are not what we will be focusing on here.

Kra and *sunsum* for the Ashanti, *eẽ* and *wawi* for the Alladian of Ivory Coast, *se* and *ye* for the Fon of Dahomey—one of these two entities always corresponds to a certain idea of stability, even personal destiny; the other to ideas of relation, mobility, influence and openness to influence. In the language of witchcraft, an individual's *wawi* is said to defend the *eẽ* associated with him or her, but it can also provide the means for an attack on the *eẽ* of another individual who is structurally tied to the first. This arrangement, which I have simplified here, refers to a double plurality, signifying the essential openness of any individual existence to existing others but also a possibly uncomfortable internal plurality. Certain Alladian healers explained to me that a strong *wawi* needed an *eẽ* that could stand up to it. Once we know that the notion of the *eẽ* also involves notions of blood and life, we can sense what is at stake: certain individuals fall ill because, afflicted with a constitutional defect, they don't measure up to the strength of their own aggressive drives. This is at any rate the diagnosis that was sometimes formulated when an individual seemed to suffer from mental disturbances: His *eẽ* was too weak for his *wawi*. The same idea could be expressed differently by saying that a good chief, a truly strong chief, must not lack nerve.

But we have not reached the end of the analysis, which can be pursued in three directions, themselves indicated by three words: ancestor, body, god.

First, there is the ancestor or, better yet, the ancestral trace. This is attentively looked for in the body of the newborn: at least one of the entities I just mentioned is always presented as a reincarnation. This does not mean we should speak of metempsychosis or individual reincarnation. What is transmitted patrilinearly or matrilinearly (and here there are numerous possible variants) is one of the elements that were once constitutive of an individuality that is now undone, dead. In using the term "ancestor" to convey the recurrence and persistence of this trace, we must specify that such an ancestor is not an individual, for the individual is never defined otherwise than as an ephemeral combination of several elements. The ancestral element is but one of these; it entered some generations earlier into a completely different combination. But its presence may be deciphered on the body, in the form of a characteristic mark or a more or less clear resemblance that deeply moves the young parents when they discover it, just as such a resemblance might move anyone, anywhere in the world.

It should be underlined that not all an ethnologist's interlocutors are equally curious about the meaning of their anthropology and the rites they practice; not all of them are equally educated, equally familiar with the exact details of their ritual. Moreover, there can be disagreement among those who do speculate about what they are doing; more often than not they are specialists (lineage chiefs, priests, diviners, counter-sorcerers). Such disagreements concern not only matters of exegesis but also points that can be considered factual, such as the direction in which a particular power is transmitted or the attributes of a given god. When it comes to human individuality, however, their thinking always follows the same course: in the multiplicity of principles that make an individual what he or she is, they distinguish at least one "identity" element and one "relational" element. We have seen that the first of these was only relatively "identitary," being in any case open to the influence of the second, "relational" one, the element constitutive of another individuality. And when this last is identified as the inherited ancestral element, we find ourselves looking at what seems like a kind of network where only the successive and respective positions of the elements, none of which is alone sufficient to constitute a human individual, matter.

Clearly we are hard pressed to apprehend in this anything that closely resembles the "subject" of Western philosophy, about whom *we* pose the problem of the relation between self and others. This comes home with full force when we learn that the most active part of the individual personality, the part that does, moves, intervenes in the lives of others, that makes history possible, as it were, may well be the reincarnated part, which cannot be assigned to any fixed, singular individual. We may also wonder how such a problematic relation of self with self is or was lived.

Far from claiming to provide answers to these questions, I shall limit myself here to clarifying the relevant incertitudes, those felt, it seems to me, by the most profound "philosophers" of ancient Africa. I shall be appealing for help in this to a commentary made by one of them, but let it first be said that the theme of identity haunts ritual practice and all practice, including of course practice that is productive of history. I have already suggested this in connection with the segmentary logic that presides over relative definitions of groups and statuses. In fact, it is as if the same logic were operating at the level of human individuality, as if individual identity were thought or conceived in the same terms as group identity—unless it's the reverse, or better yet, a combination of the two.

African ritual, to the extent that it is concerned with human individuality, seeks both to identify it (always in terms of situation, position, relation) and to fix, specify, still it, to establish its singularity. This last enterprise is by far the most difficult. The body can be the locus and the means of such fixing; it is functioning as such to some degree when it assumes the form closest to a pure object—I mean the corpse-thing, whose unique place can be marked on earth by a grave. Conversely, the body of a denounced and convicted witch may be annihilated: it is thrown into the sea or abandoned in the bush, not simply to forbid its constitutive elements from acceding to the normal paths of recomposition but also so as to make it as though it had never existed. Death is the only state in which the body can be apprehended as absolutely singular. First, as we have seen, the components of individuality are themselves corporeal. Certain specialists claim to be able to graft or transplant these components from one individual onto or into another—we could just as well say from one body to another, because the effects of such an operation are conceived to be just as physical and potentially visible to the naked eye as the ancestral trace can be. In the Agni kingdom, the king has quite literally two bodies: a slave, called the king's *ekala* (an equivalent of the Ashanti *kra*), figures the other body. The king, then, has a double body, double *ekala*, double force and double life: he who seeks to hurt him hurts the other that is within him: the other imagined as both double and lightning rod. But if the king dies, the double is also put to death. In this sense the two make only one.

The body is also the multiplicity of the organs that constitute it, express themselves in it, or betray it. In Africa it is the body's internal multiplicity rather than any sense of its unity which seems to have determined ritual practice. In all the societies of Benin, the body is made sacred through a strict delimitation of its constitutive parts. These are considered autonomous, and each is the object of specific worship. Offerings are made and unctions practiced on the organs where thought springs up (the kidneys), where the decision-making faculty is located (the head), or where anger arises (the navel). Thought, decision, anger are conceived as flowing from autonomous sources with which each individual may at very most negotiate so as to regulate the flow, master it somewhat (but what then defines the individual's individuality?). This autonomy becomes once again an identity relation founded on filiation when the organs in question—the head, or even, for the Yoruba, the big toe—are seen as receptacles of the ancestral presence.

The difference between ancestral presence and divine presence is so slight as to be almost imperceptible, not only because the gods, the *vaudoo*, are often themselves presented as ancestors, but also because a god's presence in a human being during what we call possession is akin to that of the ancestor. It is quite literally an organic presence, as we have just seen, a presence constitutive of the self and yet autonomous, constitutive of a self with which it does not merge. Bernard Maupoil was led to ask his interlocutors the following question: "To what extent does the *vaudoo* enter into you? To what extent is it not in fact your own desire that creates him?" The question did not surprise them. Commenting on the image, habit-

ual among the Fon, of a divinity that "rises up to the head" of his
faithful–the opposite, let it be noted, of imagining a god's coming
as a descent–an old man once explained to Maupoil, "Your *vaudoo*
is in your own kidney. Life does not whisper into people's ears; life
speaks in your own kidney."

Each of the categories constitutive of individuality is thus marked
by the tension between being and relation, and the figure of the god,
it seems to me, is often but the image of this tension. Gedegbe, the
Fon diviner of ancient Dahomey, suggested to Maupoil (an ethnologist lucid and honest enough always to credit his diverse interlocutors by name) extremely subtle analyses of individual identity. First,
it is constituted gradually. From the moment of birth, the newborn
is the object of procedures of identification principally concerned
with the ancestral trace; however, an individual only arrives at his
or her finished personality after a long initiation that, supposing it
does end, may not do so before adulthood. Fairly early on one speaks
of the *sɛ* (destiny, seemingly the most individualized principle), the
ye (breath, but also the strength of the relation to others), and the
jɔtɔ, which comes from a particular ancestor and will play a part, a
few generations later, in another individual recomposition. But the
complex objects that constitute the symbols associated with a particular individual (some of these objects are gods who bear a name
and are evoked in myths) are developed, fabricated, and settle into
place only gradually. Ethnologists sometimes use the expression
"personal god" to refer to this last type of object. Every human individual has his or her *du* (an essential sign that took shape on a clay
tile), *fa* (the nuts that were cast on the tile to reveal the sign), *kpɔli*
(a sack containing, among other things, a bit of the sand on which
the nuts were thrown on the day of the consultation), and *legba*, the
earthen figuration of a god placed in the bedroom of an initiated
adult and at the door to his or her dwelling. The god Legba has at
least two notable characteristics: in the bedroom he protects the individual from himself, her own passions and anger–in this case one
speaks interchangeably of an individual's anger, her navel's anger,
or the anger of his *legba*–while on the threshold of the home he de-
fends his owner against the passions and aggressions of others. This
same god Legba, reproduced the corresponding number of times,
represents all the inhabitants of the house; he also protects meet-

ings and exchanges in the market square and at crossroads: Legba is, like Hermes, the guarantor of promises. At every stage of his or her biological maturation and social development, the individual sees the material symbols of a singular identity being added to one another, constituting an identity that does not definitively settle in any one of them.

In this way, Legba is like all the other components of the individual personality: he can only be used to conceive of "one" by referring to the other. This is true not only of Legba but of the gods in general. It is also true of what would seem to be the most individual principles of personality, a fact that Gedegbe put very well when he said, "Under the name of *jɔtɔ* and with its qualities, the *sɛ* may be more readily understood." The *sɛ* is usually considered the most intimate expression of singular individuality, the individual's "destiny," whereas the *jɔtɔ* circulates, at intervals of a few generations, within the whole chronological range of an Agni lineage. Given that the *sɛ* is identified at other moments as much with the *kpɔli* as with Legba, and even with the greatest god of the pantheon, Mawu, we can see the importance of Gedegbe's conclusion and how he may have reached it. The *jɔtɔ* refers to an other which is ungraspable unless it be through its relation with *another* other. Exegesis of the god-objects used in ritual opens upon the same perspective: a god is always said to be the "messenger" of another: Fa is Legba's messenger, *kpɔli* is Fa's, or the other way around. And what matters is never the precise content of the message, only its transmission.

These objects are indissociable from commentary that may be made about them; commentaries particular to one or another diviner are in fact based on a whole series of myths and formulas that have fixed or at least traced out the shape of such divine personalities as Fa and Legba. What is true of "personal" gods is just as true of the other gods in the pantheon, which are in one sense just as "personal" as the first type. The narratives that tell of them are no more capable of stabilizing an image with which a human individual could identify in some way than is the attempt to give them material existence. This is nonetheless what is at stake in the fabrication of a god. A vaguely anthropomorphic body is made out of clay, inside of which are placed elements from the three kingdoms (animal debris, leaves, rocks), as if it were a question of summing up the matter of the world. The sum that thus comprises the statue of the god (the fetish, to use the language of the former missionaries) remains, however, singular in each occurrence. This is the paradox of the god: at one time and under the same name, he is both a mythic character in a pantheon (the hero of mythic narratives) and a multiplicity of particular actualizations.

Two remarks should be made about the paradox of the god. First, each actualization of a given god has its own particular power—each is more or less successful—because to fashion an effective god it is not enough just to follow the recipe: the priest who installs it must have certain qualities; the priest who uses it must have a certain talent and strength. A given Hevioso (god of lightning) can be stronger or less strong than another Hevioso, and the same is true for Dan, Agbwe, Sakpata (these words themselves may in some cases be taken as proper names, while in others they function as simple nouns and may be preceded by the indefinite article). However—and this is my second remark—each actualization singularizes not a particular individual but a lineage. Gods are inherited. After a particular incident, duly interpreted by the diviners, an individual may be called upon to construct or build a god, and as soon as the god comes into existence it may be transmitted, inherited. An illness can be interpreted as a neglected god's calling the successor of his former owner back to order. If we add to this the fact that very often the gods are presented as ancestors (people of the first, earliest times or, in matters connected with the dynastic chain or royal worship practices, as closer, more readily identifiable ancestors), we see that we have come full circle once again: thought about the being of being (as suggested by the fetish with its accumulation of raw materials) leads only to the staging of identity, and this identity is only expressed, above and beyond pure singularity, by reference to the others in a given relation.

So it is that neither body, ancestor, or god authorize any other definition of individual identity and singular existence than an ever-deferred, ever-asymptotic one, always subjected to the trial of events: events interpreted as signs of the other, references to an other whose singularity remains just as problematic as that of self. This game of cross-references only, and then only possibly, comes to a halt when it meets up with the figure of the witch, who is from that moment onward an unthinkable individuality and one that must be annihilated. Lineage-based Africa knew that *je est un autre* ("I" is an other) long before Rimbaud, but its answers vary as to where to look for the presence of the *other* others: the other one inherits from, the other one marries, the other one attacks, the other one fears, the other one greets, the other by whom one is greeted, and so on. The procedures and rules for identifying them are quickly incorporated; an individual is trained; one must learn to play the game, and to respect the rules of what is quite literally a *savoir-vivre*. This suggests that a culture (which is also a society) or a society (which is also a culture) could be defined as the imposed zone of consensus about *les règles du je/jeu* (*the rules of the "I"/game*)–the play on words being merely an awkward way of pointing up the necessity of having a single point of view on the singular/plural person.

In the ethnological field, the place of otherness has been displaced and in a way internalized. The others' secret, if it exists, is taken to reside in their idea–the idea that they develop for themselves (or don't develop, or develop only with difficulty)–of the "other," because determining what is other remains the simplest way of conceiving same, identical. But if this is so, isn't the others' secret our secret? And doesn't a second disillusionment then come on the heels of the first (what I've called the Romorantin effect), a second disillusionment that can then affect the certainty the observer might have of being, as far as he is concerned, *as* an observer, indifferent to what sets the observed's head spinning?

I shall not answer that question because my purpose is strictly ethnological. The relevant question here is, what becomes of the ethnological way of looking and seeing when the ethnologist comes home? To ask oneself about the meaning of one's return is, as strange as it may seem, to pose an ethnological question: what is the *chez soi*, the "home," referred to? The question is doubly inverted in that it is symmetrical to and the converse of the opening question: when one is leaving for "the others'" home, what is the others' home? And the question seems somehow to make use of the virtues of detour, circumlocution, to throw back at us and make us question the unthought-through matter of our departure. Since Montaigne, or since the eighteenth century and Montesquieu, the question has hardly been exhausted. The lessons to be learned from the detour of playing a Persian are not as obvious as has been claimed,[13] and in this they resemble the lessons of history, if only because we are never sure we know what they should be applied to or whom they claim to address.

But inverted or reverse ethnology may be so in another, more modestly methodological way. Ideally, the trajectory of an ethnologist working in "exotic" lands involved moving from the level of culture to that of the individual, even if the result was that these two terms rendered each other problematic. The ethnologist's ideal is to be distanced enough to understand the others' system *as* a system and enough of a participant to live and experience that system as an individual within it lives and experiences it. Concretely, the quest for what may be characterized as armed sympathy requires time; indeed, given that it is broken up into and over a series of individual interrelations, it is literally unending. There is no reason for me ever to cease identifying myself with my African interlocutors, no more than for me to cease identifying (and here I shall open a parentheses which I would like to leave ajar) with my next-door neighbor, my sister-in-law, or my professional colleagues. Just who or what are these proximal others who seem so familiar but whose choice of reading, beliefs, or–simpler still–whose body shape or way of carrying themselves at certain moments reveal them to me as more foreign, more distant from me, than the most distant of my African interlocutors?

This kind of ethnology is unending, but it proceeds, at the beginning, from a grasp or a progressive knowledge of the limits of the system (whether it be called social or cultural) which, on first consideration, gives meaning and coherence to individual practices. This is what Lévi-Strauss expresses so well in a curious passage from the *Introduction to the Work of Marcel Mauss*, where he analyzes the notion of "total social fact." The total social fact, he affirms, is a matter to be dealt with by anthropology, which is "a system of interpretation accounting for the aspects of all modes of behavior simultaneously, physical, physiological, psychical, and sociological." Lévi-Strauss quotes Mauss: "Only to study that fragment of our life which is our life in society is not enough."[14] From this he draws the following definition in the form of a prescription: "An appropriate understanding of a social fact requires that it be grasped *totally*, that is from the outside, like a thing which comprises within itself the subjective understanding (conscious or unconscious) that we would have of it, if, being inexorably human, we were living the fact as indigenous people instead of observing it as ethnographers."[15]

The concrete experience that can enable such understanding is first of all, according to Mauss, experience of "a society localized in space or time." Lévi-Strauss specifies that the relevant experience is "that of any individual at all in any one at all of the societies thus localized."[16] We can imagine how ethnologists' heads might spin seeing themselves assigned a task whose scope no novelist would dream of encompassing. Lévi-Strauss's own head must have been spinning, and to stop it, he took as an example of one of those "ordinary" individuals not *any* Melanesian of this or that island, but (once again quoting Mauss) "*the* Melanesian of this or that island," thus taking refuge, like Mauss before him, in a culturalist definition of individuality that was more comfortable, less grueling, than an open-ended, subjectivist one.

Reverse, "inverted" ethnology gradually traces a path in the opposite direction. It starts from what appears to be most familiar—that is, individuals—and works to detect whether and in what way their relations make up a system. The primary purpose of the interviews and life stories collected is not to enable us to understand individuals but rather to grasp the explicitly or implicitly instituted relations they have with others. At the horizon of this research, the new and problematic frontiers of collective identity should appear. But the obstacles are many. There is the irreducibility of the individual, in whom the ethnologist may readily get lost; there are also the obstacles presented by the empirical field, the field of investigation. We speak of the ethnology of the business corporation; we do ethnography in housing developments—we are right to want to do this kind of work, and it is true that we do too little of it. But the risk involved is that of confusing our empirical and intellectual objects. Perhaps it is necessary to leave the corporation or the housing development in order to understand what is being played out in them. Then there are the commonplace categories imposed by the media and current events, ethnic or generational categories that should be problematic objects of study and not its a priori framework. The best intentions can give rise to the worst ethnology—by which I mean ethnology that is the least sure of its object. Unless we consider critically the theme of the multicultural society–the term itself seems to imply that the notion of culture is self-evident and that the "multiplicity" in question has already been defined–investigation of it could bring about a serious theoretical regression, not to mention possible serious political errors.

It is perhaps here that past and present experiences may best be brought together. When speaking of cultures and ethnic groups, the most sensitive ethnologists have come to understand that they are dealing, for lack of anything better, with relative and unstable categories. This has not prevented anthropology from improving our knowledge of concrete interrelations and structural logics while honing its reflection on the categories it uses. Given that we can be more or less sure that ethnologists studying industrial and media society will be able to communicate with the individuals around them, they have a chance of discovering (at the same time as they progressively discover that each of their interlocutors is a world of imagined and symbolic relations) the levels of organization where what is meaningful for the individual can no longer be separated from social meaning and where relations make sense in themselves, levels that it will then be up to them to name or qualify. What is essential is that the categories that have been used, criticized, and finally worn out in the ethnological study of the remote not be reintroduced as contraband in the ethnological study of the close(r)-to-home.

Geography is not a sufficient criterion for defining what is close and what is distant. Africa in the 1960s was no longer exclusively lineage-based; on the contrary, it had long been haunted by the presence and influence of foreigners. Conversely, Africa today has not forgotten its lineages, even in those places where modernization has been the most spectacular. For sadly obvious reasons, this chapter could have been subtitled "Twenty Years Later," or even "Thirty Years Later." The ethnologist's profession can give one the feeling that one is never done coming home and leaving, and, like Dumas's musketeers, I have long been sparring with the same phantoms. Most of my interlocutors of twenty, even ten, years ago are dead; they were old. But in Africa there are always prophets and healers on the rise, so many potential interlocutors resuming unremittingly the same discourse, speaking of the Whites, God, economic development–history, otherness, alienation–all the while treating individuals one by one, listening to each tritely singular story, speaking alternately of bush spirits and penicillin, television and witchcraft. Without perhaps knowing it but not without sensing it, they deal with all types of otherness and alienation at once, as if they were essentially bound together. I have tried to suggest that they are right.

The reader will have seen what I'm getting at. Just as the two types of ethnology, wherever they are practiced–Abidjan, Paris, my home town–are in fact one and the same, so the cultural other and the individual other make one.

2 Others and Their Meaning

Anthropology deals with the meaning that human beings living collectively give to their existence. That meaning is relational; it corresponds to the better part of symbolic and operative relations between human beings belonging to a particular social group. To speak of meaning in the context of anthropology is to speak of social meaning.

Social meaning is not identical to the sum total represented by a cosmology or social theory; it cannot be identified with the ensemble of social rules of the game that a skillfully questioned informant can reconstitute or provide a list of. It is only actualized in particular statements that specify the relation between different partners in social life, circumstantial utterances referring to normal–that is, culturally symbolized and accepted–relations between a father and his firstborn son, for example, or a brother and a sister, a husband and a wife, a maternal aunt and a uterine nephew, and so on. This "normality" is not limited to kinship relations. One expects the behavior of all those who are partners in social, economic, and political life to conform on the whole to the types of behavior symbolized and instituted in and by their society.

We may define social meaning in terms of two ways of being related. First, every individual is related to various social subgroups; his or her class identity, in the logical (rather than Marxian) sense of the term *class*, is defined by reference to these subgroups. I'm referring to one's belonging to a group of siblings, a lineage segment, an age group, a clan, a village, a nation, and so on. But each singular individual is also defined by his or her symbolic and instituted (normal) relations with a certain number of other individuals, who either do or do not belong to the same social subgroups. In short, while there is otherness, relation, meaning within a given lineage segment, lineage, age group, nation, there can also be otherness, relation, meaning between individuals who belong to different social groups–up to the point where the distance between these groups or universes of reference becomes so great that individual differences are swallowed up in it or can only be symbolized with difficulty. We know the problems of interpretation with which discovered societies were faced when their discoverers suddenly appeared in their midst. Were they ancestors? gods? But we also know the problems that can be caused to individuals by the recomposition of collective differences in the case of war with a foreign power or civil war. It may be relatively easy to constitute Rome and Alba Longa, or Croatia and Serbia, as symbols of absolute opposition, absolute difference, but we find it more difficult to assimilate the Horaces and Curiaces[1]–a spouse, in-laws, a child of ours–to the disgraced and spurned universe thus created.

Social meaning is organized around two axes. Along the first, which could be called the axis of belonging or identity, are situated the successive memberships that define the individual's various class identities. This axis runs from the most individual to the most collective, from the least all-embracing, as it were, to the most all-embracing. The second axis, which could be called the axis of relation or otherness, calls into play the more abstract and relative categories of same and other; these are applicable to either individuals or groups. We hypothesize that the essential object of ritual activity in its diverse forms is to organize and master this double polarity, individual/collective, same/other.

Ritual activity, whose essential purpose is to establish, reproduce, or renew individual and collective identities, is thus affected by a kind of double play. Either it focuses on the pair individual/group, as in the majority of collective rites marking individual promotion from a given social category to a higher level or a collective change in status—the term ethnologists traditionally use for this is "rite of passage"—or else it calls the opposition/complementarity of same and other into question, as in the personal rites carried out at an individual's birth or death or during major events in his or her existence such as illness. In the second case, one looks closely at the inherited part, scrutinizing the ancestral element that enters into the composition of the newborn (the part of other in same), or hypothesizes the intrusion of an external element affecting the internal balance of a single individual (as in all cases of "anthropophagic" witchcraft). The identity/otherness pair refers, then, to a double opposition—individual versus group, same versus other—which itself corresponds to the twofold nature of the ritual act, for while it is unique for each person who is the object of it (one is only initiated once and this is a major event in each individual life), it is recurrent for those who are either not yet or no longer directly its object. This is the paradox of the *carnet du jour*:[2] habit and repetition arise through the daily adding together of singular events (births, weddings, deaths). It does not follow from this that the axis of identity is exclusively "social" and the axis of otherness essentially "personal." The double polarity that characterizes the identity/otherness pair suggests, on the contrary, how relative the opposition social/individual is. No one doubts that social categorization is constitutive of a person or, conversely, that the procedures by which a person is defined are socially preconstructed. Social and individual are like each other's shadows, and ritual is never more spectacularly enacted as when the illusion of the individual or collective body is effaced: either when someone dies—anybody's death is one that must be dealt with—or when the king dies, for his is a departing that must first be denied, then symbolized, and whose effects must afterwards, during interregnum periods, be conjured away. It is precisely the annihilation of the individual body, the drama of death and new birth, which is staged by certain rituals of initiation involving phenomena of spiritual possession.

All thinking about others' meaning must involve a study of their ritual activity, which may be defined as the way they handle, by way of "class" identities, the necessities pertaining to the particular system of differences that is their social system and, by way of otherness, the no less obvious but always problematic necessity of conceiving the individual in intimate relation to what he or she has not yet become or is no longer.[3] All deficiencies in the identity/otherness pair correspond to a weakening of the symbolic logic that makes relations between people possible and effective. It is just such a weakening that we witness when situations of "cultural contact" such as colonization or modernization shake up the internal structures of local cosmologies, or when, closer to home, the "intermediary bodies" whose diminishment Durkheim already deplored a century ago can no longer manage to create significant relations between people. Clearly these are phenomena with psychological as well as sociological repercussions.

We would suggest that one of the axes of ritual just defined should be placed under the sign of ambivalence and the other under the sign of ambiguity. As for the two notions, ambivalence and ambiguity, which I will presently define and distinguish, we must take into account the fact that in anthropology they can be applied both to anthropological observation itself–the relation between the observer and the object of observation–and to the interpretations of the observed: the relation that the observed-observers, objects-subjects, have themselves to the reality they have mastered, symbolized, and instituted.

To qualify a person, attitude, situation, or proposition as "ambivalent" is to postulate that it can bear contrary judgments, that such judgments are equally relevant: a given person is both good and bad, a given affirmation is both true and false. This plurality of possibilities generally implies a plurality of points of view: a good mother can be a bad wife; a good husband can be a bad father; or conversely, a gangster can be a loyal friend or have a highly developed sense of honor (much of French movie-making in the last twenty years has busied itself illustrating these moving paradoxes). Ambivalence can also refer, of course, to the complexity of feeling within a single point of view, the famous love-hate feeling, the *tu me fais du mal, tu me fais du bien* ("you hurt me, you do me good") of *Hiroshima mon amour*. In all cases a diagnosis of ambivalence implies perceiving the coexistence of two qualities, even if, in the domain of truth judgments, ambivalence is due only to a change in point of view or scale.

To affirm, on the other hand, that someone or something is *nei-*

ther good nor bad or, in the field of truth judgments, that a proposition is *neither* true nor false, is to leave ambivalence behind and enter the field of ambiguity; to put in negative form–the form considered at a given moment to be the only one possible–something positive that cannot yet be qualified. It is to postulate the necessity of a third term: to suggest, for example, that Ulysses loves neither war nor his wife but traveling, which enables him to move from one to the other.

Ambiguity does not have the same status as ambivalence. It cannot be dispelled by a change in point of view–in this sense its scientific status is less assured–but it is explicitly temporary, and in this it is scientifically more promising. Inscribed in time, it contains the promise that it will surpass itself. Every scientific theory is ambiguous in this sense because it is, and knows itself to be, temporary. It is neither true, in the sense of a truth that clarifies or illuminates all things or for which all is clear and luminous–the gaze of God–nor false, since it is from the exploration of its limits and incapacities, the refutation of its predictions, to use Karl Popper's language, that a "truer" hypothesis and theory will spring. To the extent that the ultimate purpose and end of science is, as Stephen Hawking has affirmed in his *Brief History of Time*, the discovery of a unique theory that describes the whole of the universe, only that complete theory could with any intellectual rigor be said to be true. But on the day of such a discovery, as the author puts it, "we would know the mind of God."[4]

In light of the ambivalence/ambiguity pair, what can we say of anthropology as humankind's knowledge of human beings? The answer to this question involves three notions that correspond to three levels of reflection. From the point of view of an external observer who is interested in the totality of thought systems and organization systems represented in the world, the problem of understanding involves refuting the relativist hypothesis. For the person who observes the functioning of social structures within a single culture, the modes in which authority is exercised in it, its universe of belief–a sort of observation that includes the ideas the observed themselves have about these structures and modes, this universe–the key question is that of efficacy: what make things run? Finally, for the person who wants to avoid dissociating the problems that the ob-

served experience from the problems that they raise for their observers, the central theme is that of relation as inscribed in the more
general problem of identity.

The relativist hypothesis in its most extreme form is concerned
with ambivalence, not ambiguity. It casts doubt not on the existence
of local truths, but rather on the ability of an external observer to
apprehend and translate those truths completely. And it casts doubt
on the existence of a superior point of view from which these truths
might be ordered in relation to each other. In the Pascalian and
proverbial expression, *Vérité en deçà des Pyrénées, erreur au-delà*
(What's truth this side of the Pyrenees is error on the other), the
term "truth" may be taken quite literally to mean that there are no
other truths than those we may qualify indifferently as cultural, local, or particular. A relativist ethnologist does not refuse the exac-
titude of his or her colleagues' descriptions but rather the general-
izability of such descriptions. For a relativist ethnologist, such descriptions are true, in that they correspond to a particular situation,
and false, in that if one were to pull back the point of observation,
one could not claim to inscribe them in or apply them to the new,
wider configuration.

It is not my purpose here to develop a critique of relativism, but
rather to distinguish the ambivalent conception of culture that corresponds to relativism from the theme of ambiguity that becomes
manifest within each culture as soon as that culture puts "perfor-
mative" procedures (to borrow a term from linguistics) into operation. The theme of ambiguity appeared in anthropological literature
from the moment anthropologists began to consider power and effective representations, or to describe schemata and scenarios that
are interpretive in character, as in the case of divination or witchcraft accusations. It is of course the observer who understands
things in terms of "ambiguity" in his or her effort to comprehend
the ways in which the people observed endorse or interpret their
own system. But such an observer is struggling to translate phenomena perceived and named by the observed, phenomena that in
the observer's own vocabulary usually do not fall under a single
term. A witch may be considered either harmful or useful depending on the case; one who can do good can also do evil, and like
Apollo, all healers may well be feared, for one who knows how to

heal is also one who can cause illness. The king is feared for his strength, but his weakness, when he is no more, may also engender catastrophes. These alternating possibilities would stand as a perfect definition of ambivalence if they were not expressed in and through *time*, if they were not the object of successive retrospective interpretations that, because they do not cancel each other out, become continually more complex, nuanced, rich. (I am of course speaking of local interpretations, in themselves a full object of study for ethnologists.) The good or bad sovereign, the good or bad healer can only be discussed as such *over the long term*, when one has become conscious of the fact that they are neither good nor bad but something else, something more, for which we do not really have a word; that they possess a power or a quality of which it may be said that, though it is nameable in a vast number of cultures, we can never know, even from the point of view of those cultures (because, to tell the truth, thus formulated the question cannot be answered) whether it is good or bad to possess it. Similarly, in Western societies, we consider political longevity to be proof of a strength that cannot really be qualified in terms of current morality. And when an opposition party comes to power in a democratic regime, the fact that it doesn't use quite the same language as it did when it was not in power seems to us just part of the way things are, not because politicians lie more than other people (though certain demagogues may lead us to believe this), but because we sense that this case elicits a different type of assessment than that of a pure and simple judgment of immediate truth.

If we move back and forth from the point of view of the observer to that of the observed, we risk being unaware of the point of view from which the procedures of both the first and second appear equivalent. It is surely possible to show how thinking about identity or otherness (the ethnologist's real field of observation) is as essential to the ritual activity of the observed as it is to the intellectual perspective of those who observe them. Ritual activity involving birth rites, initiation rites, diverse ways of questioning the meaning of given events, rites designed to deal with illness, misfortune, and death, all concern identity and otherness. All reflection on the "other," on others, and the possibility of interpreting their interpretations is only the other side of the question of what founds the

category "same." The (symbolic) connection between identity and
otherness—a connection whose necessity is expressed by the most
refined African rites in two ways: first, every singular identity is relative to another, inscribed in relation to others, and second, whatever the modes of the different divinatory practices, they always
manifest the existence of an individual sign, a singular formula, a
residue not exhausted by all the combinations of filiation and alliance—both provides the ethnologist with immediate material to
observe and is constitutive of his or her way of looking. This means
that what I have elsewhere called reverse or inverted ethnology[5] has
much less to do with a kind of turning back to oneself enriched from
having experienced the other than a turning back to and reconsid-
eration of the questions we have addressed to those others, whose
meaning and import we are perhaps better able to measure when we
ask them of ourselves. By trying too hard to avoid ethnocentrism,
we have run the risk of removing all substance from the others' reality, of remaining unaware that their questions are also our questions (and vice versa) and that their responses are therefore not arbitrary or exotic in a way that might make them forever foreign or
derisory to us.

Are same and other the same? I would suggest that such an affirmation is both true and false, and that it is neither true nor false:
that it is to be placed under the twofold sign of ambivalence and ambiguity. It is true *and* false in that its degree of truth depends on the
point of view taken. The segmentary model upon which Evans-
Pritchard shed so much light is always relevant if we keep to only
one of its principal inspirations, namely, the process of identification through differentiation by means of which those who are opponents at one level become united against others at another level. I'm
referring to the "unity and diversity" model that even the nation-
state readily accepts: *Et tout ça, ça fait d'excellents Français* ("And
all those [different sorts of] people make excellent French people),"
as Maurice Chevalier used to sing. The observer's point of view can
also vary, and while it is obvious that, as Lévi-Strauss affirms in
Structural Anthropology, generalizations make comparisons possible and not the other way round,[6] a generalization can itself only be
made at a level where diverse data may be considered similar.

Clearly, however, the affirmation "same and other are the same"

is also neither true nor false. We cannot deny the obvious fact of difference on the basis of which all ethnological research is constructed. Our most immediate collective situation attests to it if we
consider, for example, the difficulties involved in constructing Europe, as does our most immediate individual situation as soon as any
one of us begins to think about his or her next-door neighbors or
those (s)he considers close. Nor, moving in the opposite direction,
can we deny the obvious fact of how closely each of us resembles all
of us, the fact that founds in right and law the idea of a single humanity whose most powerful and triumphant expression is to be
found, above and beyond the vicissitudes and furor of history, in the
ideology of human rights. To say that people are like one another
and fellows is thus, strictly speaking, to utter a statement that is neither true nor false because people are first and foremost something
else—equal before the law, for example.

Observing ritual, therefore, requires us to dissociate several
points of view. What we observe in ritual is a questioning of the
world, of social reality, of the individual and relational human being. We know how to characterize the style and particularities of ritual, but its form and foundation should also be of keen interest to us
because they concern realities that are problematic for *us* too. The
work that ritual accomplishes (as far as we are able to understand its
movement and purpose) concerns, either successively or simultaneously, membership in "classes" or groups and more exclusive and
intimate definitions of the person. Belonging is more easily described in terms of identity and ambivalence because we can belong
to more than one group, while what it is to be a person is more easily
evoked in terms of difference or ambiguity because a person is never
completely reducible either to his or her self or to any "other."

If rite is mediation, its very existence introduces a kind of third
term into the relation of ambivalence conceived of as the co-presence of two terms and the relation of ambiguity conceived of as the
co-absence of two terms. At the center of each of the two axes, indi-
vidual/collective and same/other, at the point where they intersect,
rites introduce the mediation of appearance and words. So it is that
costumes mark belonging to a given group and a person's name
identifies him or her individually at the same time as it expresses
his or her link to a certain filiation. The mediation of ritual thus in-

troduces ambivalence into ambiguity and ambiguity into ambivalence by submitting the co-absence or the co-presence of the two
terms to the presence of a third term: the ritual procedure itself.
Ritual mediation has the effect of correcting through a dose of ambiguity what is substantialist and definitive in assignations of identity made in terms of ambivalence. It introduces a measure of nega-
tion into the accumulated affirmations that, taken separately, constitute ambivalence.

While name giving is partially inscribed in a logic of belonging (it
often attests to the named individual's tie to a lineage segment), ritual word is, more broadly, mediation between same and other to the
extent that it concerns the definition of the individual person. Ritual
word works, for example, to manage and elucidate phenomena of
influence or long-distance action, to stage and describe the activity
of the shaman during his waking dream, to translate into language
and social prescriptions the possession of the apparently depersonalized possessed person. Phenomena of possession associated with
initiation procedures particular to different religions (procedures
such as those we may observe in the Yoruba or Fon societies that
Bernard Maupoil and Pierre Verger, among others, have described
with such precision)[7] make, unmake, and remake the personality of
possessed initiates through a symbolic game of alternately staged
death and resurrection. The god is presented at times as descending
upon them, at times as ascending from the depths of their bodies,
and always as a distant ancestor, founder of the filiation in which
they are inscribed, with the result that, if same is defined by the
other it carries within itself, the other appears, conversely, as the
very model of the same. Of the possessed initiate we may say either
that he or she is the same *and* an other (an other and the same) or
that he or she is *neither* the same *nor* an other. This language, in
which ambivalence and ambiguity become indistinguishable from
each another, expresses the perfection of the ritual act.

3 The Proximal Other, or The Other Next Door

For some time now in Europe and more particularly in France, we have been asking ourselves whether it is possible to conduct ethnological research *chez soi* (at home) in the same way it has been done *chez l'autre* (in the other's home). First, a few remarks on these expressions, which echo current debates on the ethnological study of those close to us and on relations between the "other" and the "like."

If we postulate that ethnology is possible *chez soi* as well as *chez l'autre*, the difference between this self (*soi*) and other becomes relativized. Used as absolutes, the pronouns "self" and "other" have only relational or relative meaning; they seem to evoke the possibility of a double ethnology: an auto-ethnology, whose object would be the observer himself or her immediate circle, and an allo-ethnology, where the externality of the object would be assessed in terms of its distance—geographical, cultural, social—from the observation point or, if we will, the observer.

This second remark entails three others. First, what we mean to designate by the term *chez soi* is either Europe and the United States or, in some cases, only France. The term *chez l'autre* refers to all other places and groups living in them. Second, this "self "and this "other," even thus arbitrarily delimited, are each internally heterogeneous, and to speak of ethnology *chez soi* and *chez l'autre* does not exclude the possibility of a multiplicity of ethnologies *within* self—Breton farmers studied by Breton, or Parisian, ethnologists, for example—or *within* the other: Baoulé farmers studied by a Baoulé ethnologist, for example. Third, we know that in practical terms, and for a variety of reasons, ethnology practiced *between others*, that is, others who are studied by others, becomes more difficult as the degree of otherness characterizing the relation between the observer-other and the observed-other increases. Excellent African Africanist work exists today, but it has generally been done by African ethnologists who come from the cultural groups they study. Ethnology between others who are distant from each other—New Guinea Baruya Indians studied by Yanomami Amazon Indians, for example, or the reverse—is practically nonexistent. The reasons for these difficulties and this absence are historical, and in that sense, contingent.

The last configuration is ethnological study of self conducted by the other, or (to return to an ethno-centered language whose untenableness is demonstrated by just this way of expressing the configuration) Europe studied by ethnologists who come from regions that have traditionally been of interest to Western ethnologists: the ethnological study, in sum, of self-become-other by others-become-selves. The development of such an ethnology is obviously to be wished, in the same way that the intensifying of all exchanges, particularly intellectual exchange, is desirable for peoples who intend truly to liberate themselves from the bonds of colonization or domination. In sum, this kind of ethnology is of value for reasons that do not pertain essentially to the discipline; there would be cause for concern if it were otherwise. About twenty years ago it was occasionally said that when Africans made their contribution to the ethnological study of Africa, for example, our vision of Africa would be renewed. Thankfully, this has not been the case. The reason is not, as is sometimes said, that because of their training and prolonged stay away from the milieu of origin, African intellectuals find themselves in a situation analogous to that of European observers. This may be true, and in certain circumstances it is probably better not to be implicated—or to keep one's implication to a minimum—in the situations one observes. But that is not the question, or not the whole question, for it concerns only method. In fact, the high expectations placed on an African vision of Africa, to stay with this example, clearly sprang from an idea of what the object of that vision (and ideally of all ethnology) should be: a culture common to all members of a group; people assumed to be so profoundly suffused with that culture that only *they* are in a position to apprehend it as a totality and express its complexity. So it was that between the native's knowledge and the ethnologist's desire an abyss of difference in ways of seeing and speaking was dug out, across which the native ethnologist, able to listen to and hear himself and those close to him, would–it was hoped–someday, perhaps, throw a fragile gangway.

This was of course a highly debatable conception of culture, and beyond that, of ethnology. Furthermore, it is not impossible that those who were the most sensitive to the promise of this type of internal observation–Africans studying Africans–were also, paradoxically, the most skeptical about or the least interested in the attempts made by a few emboldened explorers to debark into modernity, to turn ethnological eyes on the industrial West and do ethnology "at home."

This first set of remarks is meant simply to remind us that behind the question we are led today to reformulate–Can we do ethnology *chez soi* like we do it, or like it has been done, *chez les autres*?–we rediscover the validity and relevance of the old methodological prescription that ethnology must be both participatory and distanced, and, behind that, the necessity of having a consistent idea of the research object. Without it we cannot speak in both cases of ethnology. At this point we are back to the problem of culture, or rather, cultures, a problem receiving renewed attention today, both in the field of intellectual inquiry, because of the vitality of American culturalism, and in politics. In France at least there has never been more talk of culture: culture as it pertains to the media, young people, immigrants. The intensive use of the word, more or less uncontrolled, is itself a piece of ethnological data.

My second set of remarks concerns the notion of identity. Ethnologists' other was first and foremost the one they crossed the seas to look for, the one who intrigued them by his difference. From "the other" to "elsewhere" and from "elsewhere" to "otherwise"–the chain might have seemed self-evident if the whole stated end of ethnology had not been to get nearer to that other, to study him in the closest possible quarters, and if the ethnologist's ideal had not been, under certain conditions, to partake of the other's view of things, to become, for a time, like him. Let us remember Lévi-Strauss's analysis of Mauss's notion of total social fact (see Chapter 2). And Mauss's own perplexity, expressed in his brief review of an article by the German ethnologist F. S. Krause, upon reading Krause's definition of *Volkskunde* (the study of peoples), a definition so broad that it seemed to Mauss to be just as applicable to sociology:

> What further increases the confusion is that he [Krause] refuses to limit his study either to civilized peoples or primitive peoples. For him, scientifically, there are no superior or inferior societies. Peoples without written histories are in no way opposed to historical peoples. *Volkskunde* deals with both types, and not simply so as to describe their individual and concrete forms but in order to establish general laws.[1]

Krause's article was written in 1899; Mauss's commentary in 1900. What Mauss reproached Krause for was not his extremely broad conception of *Volkskunde* but his distinction between "diffuse" social life (mores, popular beliefs, customs) and organized social life (constituted dogmas, codified law). Mauss asked whether diffuse phenomena can in fact be so easily "abstracted from corresponding organized phenomena."[2] The most distant other is, then, not so different as an object of study from those others who are closest to us, our predecessors on the same land or our contemporaries here and elsewhere. The Durkheimian tradition is not exoticist, and we see that certain currents of *Volkskunde* are in keeping with it on this point. For a part of ethnological Europe at the turn of the century, the Other was like God for Pascal: we wouldn't be looking for him if we had not already found him. At the very least, we wouldn't be able to get closer to him if we didn't already sense that he was very close indeed.

The notion of the unconscious, a notion quite present in Mauss's work, implies that above and beyond local particularities, we are able to apprehend the profound mechanisms that make societies comprehensible and comparable. The complementarity of psycho-analytic and ethnological assumptions and procedures throughout this century, more exactly the symmetrical and inverted character of their respective trajectories, is patent. Behind the shuttered certitudes of the Western self, Freud discovered another world, the other within the same, we might say, for the adventures and avatars of the ego refer back to its twofold origin in the Oedipus complex and the primal scene. The proximal other, *c'est moi.* Nineteenth-century French literature as a whole, attracted as it was by distant or folkloric cultures, tried its hand, in a movement parallel to Freud's, at playing with the limits of individual identity, testing the constancy and the limits of the self, either by discovering otherness in identity—*Je est un autre*, as Rimbaud put it before Lacan—or by proceeding in the opposite direction: Flaubert's *Madame Bovary, c'est moi.* Let us consider what Nerval wrote in his *Promenades et Souvenirs* (1855) on attachment to the places of one's childhood and origin: "Seeking to study the others in myself, I have the impression that much of the feeling of attachment to the land is love of family." It may be said of psychoanalysis that the movement through which it discovered the other in the same, plurality within the singular, was extended and fulfilled by the ethnological discovery of the same in the other—Freud in fact postulated this identity in *Totem and Taboo* (I am referring to the parallel he draws between phylogenesis and ontogenesis)—and more precisely by all the currents and representatives of twentieth-century ethnopsychoanalysis. Mauss almost seems to be approving this research in advance, together with Lévi-Straussian structuralism, in the following affirmation from the 1902 text, "Leçon d'ouverture à l'enseignement de l'histoire des religions des peuples non civilisés":

> Social facts in general, religious facts in particular are an external thing. They are the intellectual atmosphere within which we live, and we conceive them without willing to and above all without being conscious of the causes of our acts, as when we use a mother tongue. Just as the linguist must discover beneath the false transcriptions of a given alphabet the actual phonemes that were pronounced, so the ethnographer, with the information given him by natives, whether Oceanians or Americans, must rediscover the profound facts, those that are almost unconscious because they exist only in collective tradition.[3]

Here, using strictly Durkheimian terms, Mauss bases the unconscious character of the relation between social actors and their practices on the "externality" of social facts, designated as "things." There is certainly much to be said about the different statuses of the unconscious in the various approaches we have mentioned here. What they all have in common, however (whether or not this involves calling into question the category of same and the identity of the self), is that they postulate the relative proximity of the other.

Ethnology is symmetrical to and the reverse of psychoanalysis. It postulated from the outset that same was to be found in other, and it is presently reaching a conclusion imposed on it by its new field of research, ethnology "at home"; namely, that there is other in the same, and that this otherness corresponds to the distance necessary for any observation to be possible—a distance that is not the same as the distance one has from self in self-awareness and reflection on self. Such otherness becomes entirely empirical from the moment that we choose as object a given profession, business firm, or housing development, all of which enable us to assign certain objective limits to the group under study.[4] But things are not that simple. First, identity is always two-faced. The fact that an ethnologist can identify a given group with the housing development in which its members live or the business firm that employs them, for example, does not mean that those he is observing strongly identify *themselves* with that housing development or business firm. They construct their own identity, and that construction is twofold: within the referential universe chosen by the ethnologist, *some are different from others*—a distinction or differentiation that may be quite sharp, be it in terms of sex, job profile, ethnic belonging, professional status, or something else. A housing project or a particular firm is no more homogeneous than a lineage-based society. Moreover, neither the housing project nor the business firm constitutes a closed world. Class identities—once again, I use the term "class" in its logical sense, in the sense used by the ethno-psychiatrist George Devereux—are constructed for the most part outside the universe of workplace or housing project, though it is of course obvious that from one universe or class to another such identities reinforce or contradict each other, become accentuated or lose their sharper contours, become more complex or simpler. What, then, do the ethnologist and his or her subjects of observation have in common? The answer is, they are both looking at each other. In this nothing radically distinguishes the ethnologist's situation from that of being face to face with a radically foreign group; the ethnologist is also the

object of successive identifications made by the observed which have
to do with the place he or she takes or that is assigned to him or her
on the research site, and with the position he or she occupies (or is
imagined to occupy) in society at large. The reciprocal process of
identification—and this is surely what makes *chez soi* ethnology so
original—is carried out by means of criteria and references that are
in part *shared* by the ethnologist and those he or she is studying. I
say in part because, in various ways, they are unequally "cultured."
There are those who know more than others (as is the case, for that
matter, with group members studied by *chez les autres* ethnology).

The relative cultural proximity between observer and observed in
chez soi ethnology has perhaps the advantage of making manifest a
twofold impossibility that the prestigious remoteness of exotic cultures may cause us to ignore. First of all, it is impossible to dissociate
one of the common meanings of culture as the word is applied to individuals—what we mean when we say that someone is or is not "cultured"—from the global meaning of culture, admittedly vague, but
for the moment let us accept that it is what we mean by the word in
expressions such as "Western culture," "bourgeois culture," "Dogon culture." Second, it is impossible to dissociate the problems of
group identity from those of individual identity. George Devereux
believed that an individual's withdrawal into a single one of his or
her class identities signaled the danger of the individual identity's
utter collapse. This implies that individual identity necessarily involves the building of *multiple* identities. In fact, the building of
such individual identities is a task that all cultural systems of which
we have any knowledge work to accomplish. When joined together,
these two impossibilities define a third: the impossibility of dissociating the very notions of culture and identity. As soon as we formulate these three impossibilities in positive terms—"Culture and identity are two indissociable notions that apply simultaneously to individual reality and collective reality"—they can be seen to define the
condition that will enable us to collapse the distinction between ethnology *chez soi* and ethnology *chez les autres,* and to clarify our project of a generalized anthropology.

That project requires a reexamination of the notion of culture.
Due to what is sometimes called the acceleration of history, we are
in a particularly good position here and now to appreciate the global

character, or rather, the encompassing character, of what we call
culture–each person's individual investment in general norms–as
well as the limits of this encompassing and this investment, and,
even more keenly, the plasticity of culture, its receptiveness to influences of all kinds, its active and, if you will, historical character.
We have all heard a friend or relative at one time or another declare
about this or that contemporary cultural trait, particularly in the domain of mores, "Oh, if my grandfather had seen that! . . . If he saw
that he'd roll over in his grave," and the like. I myself have memories of Brittany in the forties, and of a Breton great-grandmother.
Even though today, sometimes as a result of voluntarist initiatives,
many marks denoting an unquestionably Breton identity live on (a
quite heterogeneous identity, but that's another story), if only because they are engraved in stone and in people's memories, it is the
changes–changes that come about progressively and "naturally,"
changes of which we only become conscious through recourse to
memory and nostalgia–that are more striking than any Breton identity. I am not speaking of massive economic and technical transfor-
mations, but of everyday life: changes in dress, how leisure time is
spent, relations between generations, sexuality, marriage, procre-
ation, and, more broadly, the relation of Brittany to French society
as a whole, to the media and political life in France. That is hardly
suprising, one may justly remark. At the most I am tempted to exclaim, with others, "Oh, if my great-grandmother could've seen
that!" Set down in–set against–this present, my great-grandmother
is an other. (She is, of course, also nothing but a memory.) In *Race et
Histoire* Lévi-Strauss brilliantly evoked the disinterest of the very
old for a time that doesn't speak to them anymore, that quite literally condemns them, before death, to silence.[5] But not everyone
ages at the same pace. Many individuals "evolve," which is to say
that they transform themselves, just as their relation to others and
the cultural conditions of this relation are transformed. Many persons who are seventy-five or eighty years old today have easily borne
the cultural revolutions of this twentieth century. It is probably not
an indifferent matter whether one was twenty, thirty, or sixty years
old in May 1968, but for people of all those ages what was at stake
for the individual often could not be dissociated from the cultural
situation of the moment.

But that's precisely the difficulty, you will say, or in any case the difference between different types of society. Cultural values evolve more quickly in a "hot" historical context. Furthermore, the individual is more a party to cultural change in societies where "the individual" constitutes an essential value. Without claiming to refute such an objection entirely, I would like to nuance it by suggesting that when we speak of others we are often victims of preconceived ideas, namely, of a certain idea of culture that could well play us false when we begin to speak of ourselves.

Today we no longer succumb to the temptation of considering the distant societies we study to be stable, historyless ensembles. On the contrary, the narratives or myths we collect there continually tell of wars, political division, flight and conquests, exchanges and borrowings. But the most tenacious—and to a certain extent legitimate (there's the rub) ethnological temptation is to distinguish, within a given ensemble that has undeniably had a historical existence, resistant sectors that for their part do not require historical analysis. Let me return to Mauss's commentary on Krause. The reason Krause's *Volkskunde* seemed to Mauss so close to sociology is that it proceeded from an observation that Mauss sums up this way: "Legends, rites, usages maintain themselves intact through the long centuries of history. They are therefore realities that science can reach, and our author has the keen feeling that they are social realities, dependent upon social conditions."[6] This permanence itself, which is the guarantee of a certain scientificity, is based on the collective character of the realities that are of concern to *Volkskunde*: "It is the study of phenomena 'particular to a people,' as opposed to the study of phenomena pertaining to the individual," as Mauss summarizes Krause. And though, as we have seen, Mauss was very critical of the opposition established by the *Volkskunde* between the diffuse and spontaneous character of social phenomena on the one hand and their organized and institutional character on the other, he has nothing to say against the opposition individual/collective, which is in his opinion the condition of possibility for any sociology.

Still, neither the permanence of the cultural in the form of legends, rites, or usages *or* the legitimacy of leaving aside individual phenomena is self-evident. The effective practice of ethnological investigation does not jibe easily with such presuppositions; it often contradicts them. Let us be clear on this point. We are not concerned here to cast doubt on the interest and legitimacy of structural studies that treat a corpus of myths or an ensemble of representations. Whatever the historical jolts and upheavals—and leaving aside the cases of social pathology of which ethnology and history sometimes seem to furnish examples—the demands of internal meaning definitively prevail, in the same way that an ordered image is composed at the bottom of a kaleidoscope shaken by an impatient hand. But intellectual or symbolic order itself moves and changes, under the influence of diverse factors both external and internal. This is to say that what is cultural is essentially and literally problematic.

Let us take as an example those rites called inversion rites to which ethnological literature has devoted numerous analyses concerning societies on various continents.[7] We can make three observations. First, regardless of whether such rites stage differences in social status or the division between the sexes, they always correspond to problematic moments: changes in season, generational promotions, interregnum periods. Second, they accentuate and even caricature differences rather than denying them. Men "load" their feminine roles, women their male roles, and the same is true of the games played around political functions. Finally, such critical lucidity leaves us with a certain doubt about the stability of ritual forms and their ever-necessary, ever-cathartic function. It is possible to see a single ritual form take on quite different meanings in social groups that are politically close to one another. Recent studies by Claude-Hélène Perrot and Henriette Diabaté (see the Complementary Sources), one on the Agni kingdom of the Indénié, another on the Agni kingdom of the Sanwi, define quite differently the role played by the slave-king's double at the moment of the king's death. Among the Indénié, the role includes an aspect of denunciation and derision that has no equal among the Sanwi. It is of little importance that this difference may be imputed to differences in size and degree of political structure or in the degree to which each kingdom has adapted to external constraints in the course of the twentieth century. The fact is that cultural matter is vulnerable and malleable. If we think of the migrations that constituted sheikdoms and kingdoms in Africa, we see that they involved acquiring numerous gods and forms of worship. When we think of the prophesying that has developed in West Africa over this century—given that it continues to develop today, it cannot be taken simply as a product of the colonial situation—we must also keep in mind that even before a Christian presence implanted itself there, very similar types of prophets had apparently been able to mobilize emotions and assemble crowds around what were then new gods and new messages that spoke of the body, illness, and misfortune—those of each individual and the people at large.

We are touching here on another problematic aspect of any culture. As we underlined above, the majority of rites that, among other things, characterize culture as such involve perfectly singular, not to say personal, matters. Whether ritual activity is practiced around birth, marriage, sickness, or death, what is being deciphered, inflected, or fulfilled through such activity is an individual destiny—even if each occurrence of the activity is inscribed in an ensemble of relations that call into play other destinies, themselves both singular and relative. The same is true of more collective and recurrent rites such as initiations. While an integral part of collective political life, they involve individual stakes, constituting a significant date in the life of a particular man or woman. The question of individual identity is intimately linked with the rites that accompany birth (giving a name, determining what ancestor has been partially reincarnated, and what the newborn's protective sign or divinity is), but individual identity is just as intimately tied to more incidental rites that, on the occasion of this or that event, may serve to measure the respective strengths of the individuals involved and assess the state of their reciprocal relations. Everyone's culture is, for each person, just such a succession of required recourses to ritual. Through them, the individual becomes conscious above all of himself, of herself, even if this new awareness has meaning only in connection with an organized set of relations.

It is one thing for the external observer to infer from these singular recourses to ritual the virtual coherence of a global system. But we often proceed in the opposite direction, substantializing a culture as a totality so as to deduce from it the reality of the individuals implicated in it. And in so doing we run the risk of attenuating the open and problematic character of culture, which depends in large

part on the tension that exists between singular questions and demands and the cultural schemata that, because they are the only
means of answering those questions and demands, inform and limit
the responses. It is a fact that in the most totalitarian (in the intellectual sense of the word) cultural systems, systems that are able to
account in their own terms for any and all events, the image of absolute individuality is unthinkable, and is for that very reason
provocative, whether it appears as the perversion of relation, as in
the case of the witch, who is necessary to the explanation of events,
or as transcending all relation, as in the case of the chieftain or king,
whose attributes are different from everyone else's and who is subject to different prohibitions. The unthinkable and challenging character of the individual would not confer on individuals the social efficacy of which we have so many attestations if everyone hadn't
tested it out first within himself or herself. For if it is true that the
individual comes to have meaning within relation, it is also true that
relation would not have any meaning without the individual. Conversely, given that identity can only be assessed at the limit of self
and other, we may affirm that that limit is essentially cultural. It
shows what a given culture's problematic points are.

I would like to illustrate this point by commenting on an author
whose conception of culture has found a sure audience in recent
years and who, as an anthropologist, is concerned not to ignore current realities, however violent or seemingly incomprehensible our
present time may be. At the very end of the chapter entitled "Person, Time, and Conduct in Bali," Clifford Geertz ponders the exceptional personality of President Sukarno (I will be pardoned for
quoting at some length):

> The emergence for almost the first time in Indonesian history of a po-
> litical leader who is human, all-too-human, not merely in fact but in
> appearance, would seem to imply something of a challenge to tradi-
> tional Balinese personhood conceptions. Not only is Sukarno a
> unique, vivid, and intensely intimate personality in the eyes of the
> Balinese, he is also, so to speak, aging in public. Despite the fact that
> they do not engage in face-to-face interaction with him, he is phe-
> nomenologically much more their consociate than their contempo-
> rary, and his unparalleled success in achieving this kind of relation-
> ship—not only in Bali, but in Indonesia quite generally—is the secret
> of a good deal of his hold on, his fascination for, the population. As

with all truly charismatic figures his power comes in great part from the fact that he does not fit traditional cultural categories, but bursts them open by celebrating his own distinctiveness.[8]

To better understand this excerpt, it is necessary to know that for Geertz the analysis of culture should involve the "searching out of significant symbols, clusters of significant symbols, and clusters of clusters of significant symbols–the material vehicles of perception, emotion, and understanding–and the statement of the underlying regularities of human experience implicit in their formation."[9] Geertz's conception of culture is neither *fixiste* or uniformalist; there can be opposition or contradiction between one group of symbols and another, and culture as a whole is said to move like an octopus, by the disjointed motions of this or that one of its parts. Certain of these parts are nonetheless united by a closer tie, and shaking one of them up is not without its consequences for those that are most firmly attached to it. After examining Balinese culture, Geertz concludes that one of these interdependent ensembles, what he calls the "Balinese triangle," consists of notions concerning personhood, time, and social etiquette, and that any new element that affects one of them will act directly on the others.

Sukarno's personality is just such a new element. Intensely present as an individual, he "ages" before the eyes of the Balinese, whereas this same people has a "depersonalized" conception of personality and a "detemporalized" conception of time. Leaving aside Geertz's analyses of the conceptions particular to the Balinese, I would simply underline the fact that for him Sukarno's personality alone (a personality nonetheless reproduced to greater or lesser degree by subordinate chiefs) deals a blow to the ensemble of Balinese perceptions just as the other two points of the Balinese triangle (time and the proprieties) are affected by particular realities of Indonesian life, the first by the continual state crisis, the second by the informal quality of urban life, pan-Indonesian culture, and youth culture.

It is clear that these hypotheses, elegant though they may be, have only a very general explicative value; they are hardly specific and may even be called weak. At the most they make possible suggestive retrospective readings that are closer to general comments than anthropological analysis. So it is that at the end of "Deep Play: Notes

on the Balinese Cockfight," Geertz goes so far as to affirm that
though the December 1965 massacres—between forty and eighty
thousand Balinese were killed by other Balinese—were not actually
caused by cockfights, they nonetheless appear to us less surprising
because of what cockfights have to say about Balinese life.[10] Considering culture to be a set of texts that "say something of something"
is to expose oneself to the risk of making them utter *anything*,
namely, truisms.

According to Geertz, who touches here on a fundamental point,
the exceptional figure of Sukarno affirms itself as external to the
schemata of traditional culture. Let us note that while "charismatic" personalities mark their difference in this way, highly instituted systems try to control and limit just such marking of difference. This detour is made possible and in fact imposed on them by
the very particular status of the individual image. Remarkably, ethnological literature tended to reserve a separate fate for the notion
of the individual person. The person cannot in fact be considered a
"part" among others making up the "sum" that is culture. The term
"person" is itself perilous because, though it has the advantage of
referring to a common conceptual schema, it proceeds from an ab-
straction incapable of expressing in turn the complexity of those
scenarios in which the personality and identity of each person are
experienced. Such scenarios, which are a good deal of what ritual
activity amounts to, implicate the whole of the given culture understood as coextensive with the social as representation. What accusations of witchcraft, divinatory procedures, and ritual activity in
general teach us, it seems to me, is that everyone "learns" *simultaneously* general and particular, essence and existence, the order of
things and the place he or she occupies in it. The concrete person
can only actualize and fulfill himself or herself within the social, economic, and political dimensions that assign that person his or her
limits. He or she is not the whole of culture but rather wholly culture, in the complex and full meaning of the term.

This is to say that the particular difficulties of ethnological investigation, about which much has been said, can indeed be useful to
the extent that we do not confuse questions of method with the
question of the object. It is true that information sources vary and
that in certain ethnological texts (once the work of writing has been

accomplished) it is hard to distinguish a pure account of local exegeses from authorial interpretation. This defect is, however, not
that widespread, and "naturalized" description of societies is tending to disappear (Geertz's Balinese were produced in part by such
description). It should nonetheless be noted that the best ethnography does not involve simply collecting information from particular
informants on general themes, but rather observing individual and
collective practices and collecting utterances or statements that are
not opinions about or information on the given society in general
but about a singular life in the process of being lived–without which
there would be no participatory ethnology. If it is indeed true that a
culture is "an open-ended, creative dialogue of subcultures, of in-
siders and outsiders, of diverse factions," to quote James Clifford
(an affirmation that Geertz would not contest), it is also the result
of singular initiatives that find in it their field of expression, their
language, and their limit, and which "work" that culture, kneading
and penetrating it, just as culture "works" the very bodies of individuals. Into the baroque character of the investigation passes something of the baroque character of existence and of culture in action,
culture in the singular-plural.

It is this quality that should make us optimistic about the future
of ethnology "at home." Two types of objections may be made to
such ethnology, which I will now formulate and attempt to refute.

The first type of objection involves the size of observable units,
and it is all the less justified in that these units may be selected in a
manner no less arbitrary than for a more traditional context. It is not
that there are no contextual differences between *chez soi* and *chez
l'autre*–it would be unreasonable to claim so. Rather, what must be
kept in mind is that the ethnological ideal has never been to delimit
representative samples of a presupposed totality. On the contrary,
only after fully exploring particular situations can we raise the issue
of possible connections or generalizations.

The other type of objection pertains to the highly differentiated
and complex character of modern, or postmodern, societies. Above
and beyond the fact that this objection would seem to render absurd
all lamentations about the globalization of culture and the stan-
dardization of mores, it unwittingly describes a type of situation that
is equally relevant for the societies that have traditionally been of in-

terest to ethnologists. The two types of objection constitute the negative, as it were, of a certain image of traditional ethnology and its
objects, an image for which the relevant words are "totality," "homogeneity," and "expressivity"; an image that no one would defend
in its entirety today and which ethnology has been able to defend itself from, if not rid itself of. It is an image that still lurks in our representations, in the camera obscura of our minds.

I would venture to say of ethnological study today and at home not
only that it is possible, but that it's necessary: it is a duty. We all
carry around in our heads these days the theme of the multi-ethnic
society. Only a dynamic conception, attentive to the "work" of sin-
gularities, is capable of giving an account of, and accounting for,
this society's present, of enabling us to imagine its future. Nothing
could be more disastrous, intellectually and politically, than vague
and lazy references to the so-called multicultural society–that is, to
cultures conceived of as closed and complete totalities, objects, according to the circumstances, of respect, boycott, or exclusion. But
if it has become necessary today to use the expression "emergency
ethnology," once reserved for observation of the world's last "savages," this is in order to underline the urgent necessity of measuring the formidable mechanisms of artificial identity production, collective as well as individual, which our societies are putting into operation. Class identities in Devereux's sense of the term, "crutch"
identities, are either being exacerbated by the media, which in
France make dangerous use of big descriptive categories–the
beurs,[11] the immigrants, the Muslims, the executives, the civil ser-
vants–or, on the contrary, they are melted down into even more ex-
tensive categories, such as "gender," "generation," "nationality,"
or "civilization." These, combined with the idealized images incessantly submitted to us of femininity, virility, or youth, constitute a
host of simple, simplistic, and dangerously loaded models. Likewise,
economic power has never been so exalted as it is today, or so intimately associated by word, image, the very reality of facts, to current conceptions of the person, the body, sport, the relation to the
other–in one word, life. I do not claim with these extremely general
observations to develop a program and objects of research but
rather to say why it is imperative to develop them.

Without becoming confused about essentials or underestimating the benefits accruing from democracy and respect for human rights, we may affirm that liberal societies insure that their members are provided with a kind of key-in-hand freedom that hardly leaves them any choice of locks. The pressure of individuals' expectations in these societies is nonetheless perceptible, sometimes manifest, and even sometimes effective. That a liberal society should also be a class society (in the Marxian sense of the term this time) is something that everyone can experience for himself or herself, and formal democracy has the substantial advantage of authorizing and enabling this coming to awareness. This is a crucial reason why ethnologists must not leave the monopoly of meaning, the deciphering of the social, the definition of same and other, of order and disorder, what is reasonable and what is unreasonable, what is normal, functional, and irrational, to improvisers. Not that on all these points ethnologists as such have much more to contribute than questions. But their contribution is the more significant in that they have an idea, gained through experience, of the way in which answers to such questions are ordinarily developed, proposed, and imposed.

4 The Others' Norm

I would like first of all, with the help of this chapter title, to reformulate the paradox constitutive of ethnology, a paradox it has not finished debating and with which it has not finished struggling. We ask of ethnology that it enable us to understand the others' culture, other cultures, both from within and without, that it be simultaneously participatory and distanced. This prescription, which pertains to method, is in fact very closely tied to a precise conception of the object, regardless of whether the former commands the latter or derives from it. Ethnology's object as it has been generally accepted for the last century is culture, culture understood as an ensemble of specific values that entail specific behaviors. Admittedly, different schools of thought have developed and used different definitions of culture. In Chapter 1 I noted two major inflections of the core definition: on the one hand, culture as an ensemble of "traits" that are technological as well as institutional (the bow and arrow, horticulture, matrilinear organization)–culture, that is, as a sum total coextensive with the whole of the social; on the other, culture as a regrouping of singular values that cannot be attributed to economic and social determinism within a given society–culture as supplement to the social. From the point of view that is ours here, culture in all cases defines a collective singularity: collective in that it corresponds to what a number of people share; singular in that it is what distinguishes them from other people.

Whether it is taken as sum of or supplement to the social, culture thus understood is both normal and normative. For those born into a given culture, it is the very order of things, an order that is thought of as imposing itself through a kind of immanent power. This is why we often conceive of the others' culture as natural. More exactly, ethnology accounts for a certain number of local givens—formal statements or regular behaviors—that seem to enclasp a society (in turn defined by that enclasping *as* a society) in a double grid of intelligibility: each society has its own norms for interpreting the real, and it is in relation to those norms that Western or Western-assimilated ethnologists themselves mean to interpret it. The Bambara or the Baoulé—the collective singular form expresses the supposed uniformity of the culture under discussion—is precisely that person or that group characterized by a particular conception of heredity and inheritance, a particular relation to the land, a particular idea of filiation, and so forth—in sum, a certain relation to the real in the absence of which neither the term "Bambara" or the term "Baoulé" would have any meaning.

The problem for the ethnologist, and even more so for the anthropologist if we make the defining characteristic of anthropology its comparatist vocation, is to know whether he or she can approve of and apply a conception of culture that is at once so all-embracing and so discriminating. It is a conception, we should note, that runs the risk of relativizing deviances just as much as cultures ("to every culture its deviances"). It could stand as the height of cultural relativism, pushing us to declare that what is crime or insanity for some is not so for others; or, conversely, it could insist that we measure each culture by the yardstick of another—our own, or what we presume to be our own—especially in what are discreetly called cultural-contact situations. In the second case, we would be guilty of ethnocentrism, where other cultures become nothing more than so many approximations or deviances in relation to the values *we* claim to incarnate.

Three remarks before we consider certain questions that may justifiably be asked on this point. First, whatever we may mean by the term "culture," it designates a real object, a reality. The word does not perhaps enable us to apprehend and measure that reality exactly, and some have sought to name it with other words; I am thinking particularly of Castoriadis's *imaginaire social*. The designation "culture" is a response to the fact that globally, statistically, and, for common mortals, intuitively, there are differences in attitude and behavior between different human groups, differences in mentality, as is sometimes said, whose existence it would be unthinkable to deny, even if the awareness we may have of them in certain contexts springs from and is conditioned by fear and distorted ideas.

My second remark concerns the timeliness of such a debate about culture. In France today, a substantial part of the population delights in practicing *anthropologie sauvage*, untutored "wildcat" anthropology analogous to the spontaneous practice of psychoanalysis in everyday exchanges. They are open to the influence of a discourse that, starting with the theme of cultural specificity, ends up establishing a near-synonymity between the terms "immigrant," "deviance," and "delinquency." The "multicultural" society energetically proposed and demanded as a counter-reference by those who justly oppose the former vision as xenophobic and racist carries with it a problem of imprecision–what exactly are the cultures of "multicultural" society?–and the very conditions of its appearance are problematic and troubling. We didn't talk about a multicultural society in France when the Polish or Italian immigrants came, for example. Even when it is formulated in the most generous terms, then, today's debate reserves a special fate for Black Africa, Arab countries, the Middle East, as if (and this could hardly come as a total suprise to an ethnologist) a certain image of European identity that is surely not its most glorious was in fact taking shape negatively; that is, by opposition to the more or less blurred image of a culture conceived both globally and vaguely as essentially different from that in which the European countries, more or less clearly, recognize themselves. Let the following observation suffice: for anthropologists, the time for indulging in the intellectual convenience of white-gloved cultural relativism is over.

My final remark is more personal and is meant as an admission of a certain uneasiness. There have regularly been discussions in France about excision. Though public opinion is often poorly informed about the various practices covered by this term (certain descriptions of infibulation have caused some confusion), everyone agrees, first, that excision constitutes an assault on the individual person, and second, that there is no reason for a law-governed state such as

France to allow excision as legitimate within its territory. Above and beyond strictly legal argumentation, certain newspapers have developed a more globally normative thesis: there is no reason to defend a given practice in the name of respect for all cultures when that practice undermines the integrity of the human person. It is indeed necessary to move beyond the strict framework of cultures as autonomous ensembles condemned to coexistence if we want to be able to speak in the name of a broader normative ideal, whose object is then the human being in the sense of "human rights"; that is, the individual as a rights-endowed being. And if we don't want to reduce this demand itself to a cultural particularity by accepting the idea that the only kind of deviance is intracultural deviance (to each his norms and deviants will be well protected),[1] it is necessary to free ourselves from an attitude of absolute respect for "cultures" in all their variety and relativity–or rather, it is necessary to relativize that relativity. Nonetheless, I have at moments been profoundly shocked by utterances that, as antirelativist as I am (I'll come back to this), I could only feel were humiliating for the women and girls about whom they were made. A practice is of course not justified in the absolute because it has meaning within a given culture, and I am not among those who think that intracultural meaning should be the last word and the ultimate object of anthropological research. But we cannot *not* take into account meaning thus conceived; we cannot decree that it doesn't exist. It exists both historically and sociologically, and what calls it into question, when it *is* called into question, is not any obvious absolute and necessary truth but rather the historically induced possibility of raising new, problematic issues, a possibility resulting from contacts or confrontations between peoples which are also contacts and confrontations between cultures in the totalizing sense of the word. I will come back to this point, which is central, but for the moment let me simply reaffirm an uneasiness that arises from an obvious cause: if it was painful for me as an Africanist–to say nothing of the African women and men who confided their feelings to me on this–to hear or read words denouncing the barbarity of excision, this was not out of hostility to their meaning or as a culturalist reaction but rather because, taken out of its context and thus invested by another, an institution such as excision (there are others that would have produced the same effect) was necessarily presented and understood not merely as cruel and even scandalous, but above all as absurd, *abnormal*. It had been integrated into a frame of reference in which it could only be affirmed to be deviant and monstrous. And this misappropriation could only be experienced as painful by those Africans who may legitimately consider that *they* are in charge of the problem, that the battle against excision is theirs to lead, but who nonetheless have no reason to consider *insane* the people—mother, father—who brought *them* into the world.

A culture is perhaps not reducible to the singular semantic totality that ethnological tradition has often wanted to see it as, but that totality exists, and even the least relativist ethnologist must acknowledge it either intellectually or affectively. The paradox of anthropology I underlined at the beginning of this chapter, which can be expressed either in terms of the object—"Cultures as totalities are different from each other, but they can only be understood if they can be compared"—or the method, which claims to combine participatory observation with a distanced eye, can only be resolved at the cost of deepening our notion of culture. Perhaps that part of the notion represented by the pair norm/deviance will provide us with the means of going deeper. In any case, reaching a profounder notion involves recognizing both the obvious fact of cultural differences and the problematic character of any one culture.

Cultural differences are, in effect, obvious. They are exemplarily expressed in different cultures' distributions of the normal and the abnormal or forbidden. In relation to the norms it institutes, every culture recognizes deviances and stigmatizes deviants. This process of internal discrimination is different from that which consists in rejecting outward and far into the distance practices deemed horrible or unthinkable (such as cannibalism in regions where it is not claimed to be honorable under certain conditions). In our own history and tradition we find ways of distributing essential values that seem surprising or shocking to us now. We know how hostage-taking has been viewed in France in the recent past; I'm referring not so much to acts by means of which a few gangsters in trouble try to save their loot and skin as to those acts that certain armed groups have claimed responsibility for in the name of revolutionary justice, the people's rights, or Islamic resistance. We react above all (and I include myself in this) against what we see as the cowardice and injustice of the act. The cause defended by the kidnappers seems to us irrevocably compromised by the means they use. We can imagine that for the kidnappers themselves the act and the extortion that follow it are a means like any other to bring about the success of a cause deemed by them to have absolute priority. But our norms are not the same as theirs, either in terms of how we judge the immediate event or what norms we desire to see operating in society. For Islamic terrorists, hostage-taking is a means to changing norms; in today's West we accept it only as a metaphor (we can say, for instance, that a politician is "held hostage" by his allies). In the Middle Ages in France and Britain, hostage-taking was first and foremost an economic transaction.

Let's listen for a moment to Jean Froissart in the *Chronicles* on the subject of his trip to Béarn.[2] The Hundred Years' War began in 1337; he tells the story in 1390; he is discussing the last quarter of the fourteenth century. As a consequence of the conflict between France and England and various local disputes, armed bands have formed who work for themselves while invoking a more elevated patronage, to whom they pledge an uncertain loyalty: France, England, Armagnac, Navarre. The "high deeds" of which Froissart speaks ("taking and pillaging castles and fortresses") would also be the ideal of Jeanne d'Arc's companions, and they are in keeping with the rules of "courtesy." In his evocation of valiant men of the time, Froissart does not entirely confuse a sovereign lord like the Earl of Foix with virtual highway bandits like Louis Robaut or Limousin. On the contrary, *their* likes would not exist if the nobility fulfilled its role, and if so many French lords were not being held hostage in England. Still, all obey the same code. If they prefer not to kill their defeated adversaries, this is out of economic interest rather than human feeling: prisoners are spared in the hope of obtaining ransom; courteous war was based on credit. The only intolerable deviance consisted in not keeping one's promise. King John, whose ransom had cost France so dearly, returns to England to die out of respect for the promise broken by his son sent as hostage in his turn. The Earl of Artois cannot forgive his brother-in-law the King of Navarre for not having paid the fifty thousand francs he made himself liable for in Lord d'Albret's name. What went counter to the rules of courtesy was not extortion, hostage-taking, ransom-collecting, or violence but breaking one's promise, for only by keeping it was war made possible and profitable.

In this context, then, and from the point of view of which Froissart is the exemplary spokesman, there are three kinds of deviants: those who break their promise (King John's son and the King of Navarre); noblemen who fail to fulfill their role of protecting dependents—as we have suggested, a large majority of the French nobility were unable to fulfill that role in those times, while, conversely, a man as harsh and cruel as the Earl of Foix enjoyed great prestige for protecting his retainers from extortion—and finally the peasants themselves when they rebelled, the *Jacques*, who didn't know the rules of courtesy ("bad people gathered together without leaders or armor") and had to be brought to a finer awareness of the rules of the game by blooded lords and adventurous captains united for the occasion.

I have used this example not so as to wonder at the fact that specific values (specific, at the very least, to a particular if composite group) correspond to a given state of social-political-economic organization (disorganization in this case), but because it clearly demonstrates that behind the reciprocal relations between normal and abnormal, or constituting those relations, the important thing is the articulation of means with ends. There is nothing unintelligible to us in the world of frenzied activity, violence, courtesy, and negotiation, of nobility and dire poverty, that Froissart depicts; we can grasp its ins and outs fairly readily. Neither is there anything in that world that would be acceptable in terms of our own norms today. We see in it instead the positional permutations of honor and dishonor, ends and means, their inversion, as it were, in relation to our official representations. Froissart's *Chronicles* belongs to our history, but let it be said in passing—and if I may be forgiven the anachronism, the fiction—it is obvious that the French governments of recent years would have as much difficulty dialoguing with the Earl of Artois as with Islamic Jihad revolutionaries.

This brings me to another example, once again more personal. It has to do with a matter about which the best and the worst has been written: witchcraft, and in this instance, African witchcraft.

Let us begin with an anecdote that goes back about twenty years. The scene takes place in Ivory Coast, in the village of Grand-

Jacques, Alladian country, on the slim, sandy cordon of land that separates sea and lagoon, about a hundred kilometers west of Abidjan. I am attending a funeral service. As usual, the people are reenacting the scenario of the multiple investigations that followed the death of the person whose funeral is being celebrated; he died a few months before. The funeral, you will have understood, is not a burial service, but comes only much later, when all the circumstances of death have been elucidated. Death is often imputed to the action of another, sometimes to a mistake on the part of the victim, who is then considered a victim of his or her own negligence, and most often to both, because the action of another is reputed more destructive when it has been allowed or actually aroused by the weakness or blindness of the one who undergoes its effects.

In the case at hand, the accused has acknowledged his guilt. By this we mean that he has admitted having attacked "in double"[3] the man whose funeral is being celebrated today. He belongs to the same matrilineage as the dead man; the inquiry (whose details I won't go into here) had brought to light that he was jealous of his future victim. A goodly number of elements gathered together and retrospectively reinterpreted have made credible the postmortem scenario and diagnosis which the social structure authorizes and in a certain way requires. Witchcraft power in matrilinear Akan societies is in fact one of the attributes of matrilineage. It is exercised within a given lineage and, according to the local anthropology, as a property of a given element constitutive of the person, it aims at and attacks another such element. It is in a way the maleficent expression *inside* the lineage of the necessary relation that unites people, and this maleficent mode is itself a fact of structure. It is inconceivable for a lineage not to include and shelter—in the person of at least one of its representatives, often the oldest or most prestigious—a power that is also the sign of its strength to the extent that it remains an object of silent suspicion. Traditionally, pushing the procedures of inquiry and accusation to their fatal issue—the death of the accused—is avoided as much as possible, though where I was living this actually happened fairly frequently. In the case that interests us here, the affair had been settled amicably, the offended party—the victim's paternal relatives—contenting itself with the accused's confession and apologies from the maternal relatives.

The preceding episodes, then, were being acted out at the funeral celebration (with a paternal relative playing the role of the deceased), and we came to the scene of the accused's admission. That day, moved by some passing whim, instead of renewing his confession at the appropriate moment as expected, the accused retracted it, affirming simply that he wasn't present in the village during the illness and death of his supposed victim. After a moment of astonishment everyone burst out laughing, and I too found myself smiling: any Alladian knows that witchcraft power can be exercised at a distance. The element endowed with that power moves away in the night while the body is sleeping; memory of dreams is but the memory of this nocturnal wandering. I was smiling myself (and I soon felt sheepish about that smile) because the accused obviously had no illusions about the poor quality of the disculpating proof he was trying to establish, in which he himself did not believe. He didn't insist, and, his brief and unreasonable fit of deductive logic behind him, he discreetly confirmed his confession and his fault. The funeral celebration was concluded without incident; dead and living were calm once more.

The universe in which this story took place is one where the activity of recognition overrides activities of knowing. I have already given some indication of what could be called Alladian anthropology, the Alladian representation of the body, identity, and relation (see Chapter 1). Anthropologists are always dealing with already symbolized universes that are nonetheless not texts (contrary to what Geertz has affirmed of cultures) because the "reading" that can be done of them is a function of the place occupied within them by the particular "reader." The reading of all these readings, the meta-reading, is a construction that only becomes a text when the ethnologist's pen makes it one. As for the partial readings of the actors, which are both incomplete and partisan, they are less readings than decipherings oriented toward prevention and action. And they are limited by an a priori conception of what is thinkable or possible. In Alladian society it is unthinkable for a father to attack his son through witchcraft—or rather, the only way to think such a thing would be to imagine substitutions and complicities (on the side of the son's matrilineage) that would complicate the scenario. Or else it would be understood that the father was not attacking his son through witchcraft but rather had cursed him, a scenario that brings different partners into play or at least assigns them different roles.

Funeral ceremonies are held at precisely the moment when all has been recognized and acknowledged. The interpretive scenarios are obviously not innumerable; far from it, given the restrictions imposed on definitions of the possible and the thinkable. What exactly is recognized, acknowledged? Signs—but anything can be a sign, and all signs are ambivalent. Illness can be a sign that the sick person is being attacked or that the sick person himself or herself has made an unfortunate assault on another; good health can be the sign of peaceful relations with one's surrounding circle or a remarkable aptitude for feeding on others' blood. A spoken word to all appearances innocuous can afterwards be interpreted in one way or another as a function of the events that followed its utterance. Such interpretive scenarios, only *relatively* diverse, need only be compatible with the universe of meaning, the symbolic universe, in which they are inscribed. This is to say that everything can be explained—the same and its opposite—but also that everything must be brought back into relation with a certain number of principles; these are present, in one way or another, in every interpretation. This circular effect is imputable to a totalitarian conception—"Everything is a sign"—that leaves no room for error or ignorance, a conception within which truth is not to be proved but discovered.

Indeed, in a universe of this type nothing can be proved. But the accumulation of signs to be scrutinized by means of a single interpretive grid entails a certainty, a conviction, which, because of the essential ambivalence of the sign, is then nourished by all the signs that the profusion of the outside world offers. We might even suppose that by the end of the chase—in which the person accused of witchcraft at times turns around and frontally contests the interpretation of signs marshaled against him, before being in a way overtaken by the event and the others' interpretation—the accused is often convinced himself: he has fallen into the trap of a world where intention is the equivalent of action and dreaming is for all intents and purposes the same as waking, a world where a word's meaning may change from the moment one finds oneself caught in the others' gaze and recognizes oneself there.

Investigative procedures in this universe of recognition and acknowledgment involve a twofold use of the logic of the sign. The interpretation of signs constituting sickness and death involves the production of new signs. When a corpse carried by members of the same age group as the dead person is questioned, the steps of the body-bearers forward and backward in response to the questions asked constitute affirmative or negative answers to those questions. Trials by ordeal are meant to measure on the body of the person subjected to them the validity of an accusation and the innocence or guilt of the accused. In extreme cases, it is the death of the accused, doubling that of his supposed victim, that confirms his guilt. In other contexts, the diverse divinatory procedures that involve an arbitrary throw of kola nuts or cowries expose configurations (signs that have been repertoried) that, once recognized and deciphered, provide a strict guide for interpreting events whose very occurrence had the value of a sign.

Not suprisingly, these worlds of sign and clue, these cultures where a good part of ritual activity tends to reconstitute scenarios around the fundamental events of illness and death, readily make us think of detective literature. Both take off from the same point, ask the same question–whodunnit?–and in some cases follow the same itinerary. In detective writing we can distinguish two types of investigative itineraries. Certain writers, from Edgar Allen Poe to Agatha Christie by way of Arthur Conan Doyle, assign the investigator the job of establishing proof of guilt by accumulating evidence, comparing testimonies, and analyzing the situations encountered. Others, of whom George Simenon is probably the most spectacular example (Simenon's style of investigation may well have its origins in the Balzacian novel), discover the warp and woof of every possible scenario within a particular milieu. Simenon's Maigret is the epitome of the participatory ethnologist. He soaks in the spirit of the place–sometimes quite literally, for every cultural milieu has its alcohols–convinced that at the end of this operation, if he can bring it to an end, the truth will simply unveil itself. And the culprit (whose identity a novelist working with this type of scenario does not seek to dissimulate) watches a bit dumbfounded, then fascinated, as the stranger-detective penetrates his most intimate environment, until the moment when, knowing himself found out, recognized, he can no longer even imagine escaping that recognition.

Let me add that the opposition just sketched between these two types of detective investigation is relative. For Agatha Christie, or rather for her hero Hercule Poirot and her heroine Miss Marple, the particular human nature evoked is often that to be found in villages and towns more or less on the outskirts of London. We can't very well imagine Miss Marple or even the strange Belgian with his very French vanity operating in a universe or social milieu other than the petty or middle bourgeoisie, marked by its memory of the splendors of colonial life. Outside the tight circle of these social relations, Agatha Christie's hero and heroine would be sorry figures, and are occasionally shown as such. Christie is definitely what may be called a regionalist writer.

We have other attestations of this secret sharing between the detective universe (that is, the universe of the detective novel) and the ethnological one. In recent years, historians and ethnologists have developed a new genre, the explicitly ethnological detective story. In addition to Robert van Gulik's famous Judge Dee, there is the rabbi-investigator working in the American Jewish milieu, and now a Navajo police detective more qualified than his colleagues to investigate what goes on in his milieu of origin,[4] and these are not all. These writers seem to have in common the presupposition that understanding a "cultural universe" necessarily entails discovering (revealing) the twists and turns of individual lives. In these discoveries it is not mainly deductive procedures per se that are at work but rather the simple observation that the truth of the whole is also that of its parts. In detective language, the guilty party is not marginal or exceptional within his milieu; he is its quintessence, and he can stand as the expression of that milieu precisely because he recognizes himself in it.

There is surely much to be said about the definition of culture implied by this genre variation. The idea that a society is an ensemble of individuals who recognize themselves in a given culture of which each is no more than an expression is, as we have said, simplistic and potentially dangerous; all ethnological and historical experience refutes it. But the fact that such an idea exists is a reality that, on the contrary, can hardly be refuted or objected to. It corresponds to the temptation felt by people in groups to constitute universes of recognition for themselves (see Chapter 5).

The unfortunate protagonist of the episode I recounted earlier was not conceived of as a deviant strictly speaking; more exactly, he was an "instituted" deviant, foreseen and implied by the structure. He was the one assigned by that structure to be an explanation of misfortune. In Alladian country this idea was expressed by saying there was at least one witch in each matrilineage. The witch, a social deviant in that during a singular episode he takes concrete form in the figure of a particular individual moved by various procedures to confess, corresponds at the same time to the summit of the intellectual norm according to which every biological event must be associated as frequently as possible with a human will. This ambivalence is exemplarily expressed in the figure of the lineage chief, who is both the first to be suspected—because the kind of thing that happens requires a strong man capable of attacking others and defending himself—and the last to be accused, precisely because he *is* strong and because it would be madness to cast blame on him rashly. This status is endorsed, moreover, by the legal sort of prescription according to which the lineage chief alone has the right to permit or prohibit questioning of a corpse, a procedure that necessarily leads to casting suspicion on someone or making an accusation.

It follows that in the episode under consideration here, the accused's going back on his confession made him doubly deviant. First there was the relative (and relational) deviance that made him the institutionally sanctioned guilty party; second, the intellectual deviance that momentarily drew him out of the frame of commonly accepted references, out of the interpretive schema that implies a conception of the person and a representation of lineage and alliance structure that are, in principle, shared by all, guilty parties and victims alike, accusers and accused, strong and weak. This attempt to put himself "outside the game"—an attempt punished by the audience's laughter—prefigures a situation that is in fact fairly frequent. I'm referring to the summoning of Western-type laws in order to apply them to lineage-type situations. We even come across African judges who become intensely uncomfortable when their work requires them to pronounce on the guilt of "aggressors" who are defined by the plaintiffs as such according to the witchcraft norms of "in double," or, conversely, on a plea of self-defense made by entirely real murderers who are apparently just as entirely convinced that they only killed in order to defend themselves from a witchcraft attack. The impossible dialogue that ensues between judges on the one hand and plaintiffs and defendants on the other—similar to that which opposes rather than brings together doctors and patients—reflects the irresolvable confrontation between two different conceptions of norm and deviance.

We recognize here both the starting point for all relativisms and the point from which all relativisms relativize each other. Taken as wholes, cultures are simply not made to engage in dialogue with one another, and this is so for at least two reasons. First, if cultures could speak, they wouldn't speak the same language; second, very simply, they can't speak, except metaphorically. People "speak" cultures—or they speak about them, either directly or indirectly through their practices—but no single one of them "says" a culture in its entirety. The totality is instead forever being reconstructed by external observers, and sometimes by a few local specialists who reflect philosopher-style on the meaning of their rites and myths. But it happens that as a result of particular situations—those in which deviances recognized as such become manifest—individuals and groups refer more or less explicitly, more or less consciously perhaps, to a totality of this sort. A sick African who knows that at the hospital they won't take into consideration all the parameters of his trouble will turn toward the person who, in his or her eyes, has the best grasp of the semantic totality within which that trouble can have meaning. That person is the healer or the prophet, with whom he or she shares a certain idea of meaning—just as, in a context closer to home, the psychoanalyst and his or her client may have certain references in common from the start.

Phenomena of cultural resistance at the group level partake of this same demand for meaning, a demand whose manifestations have been studied by authors such as George Devereux in instances of what he has called "antagonistic acculturation." But they also demonstrate the remarkable plasticity of cultures, even when cultures are considered from without as signifying totalities. Antagonistic acculturation, as Devereux explains in *Ethnopsychoanalysis*, may take three forms:

    1.   Defensive isolation, of two possible types: the pure and simple suppression of social contact, such as we see in "silent barter" between groups that are foreign or hostile to each other (in Africa, Malaysia, the Philippines) or suppression of cultural products by boycott, embargo on exports, or a combination of the two;

    2.   The adoption of new means in the milieu of origin without adopting the ends connected to them—a process that is often at work in situations of colonization or domination;

    3.   "Dissociative negative" acculturation, which is at work in the adoption of new "culture complexes deliberately at variance with, or the opposite of" the life techniques of the group from which the influenced group (or "out-group") wishes to dissociate itself.[5]

Clearly, certain aspects of present-day radical Islamism arise from an ostentatious will to stand in contrast to Western usages in the field of mores. Devereux cites examples in which the return (recourse) to an idealized past is effected "by means of techniques borrowed from, or influenced by, the culture whose very influence this process purports to negate."[6] So it is that the "Ghost Dance Religion" is "replete with culture traits and ideas borrowed from Christianity and used as a *means* to a native Plains-Indian cultural end."

    Such play with means and ends, which may well lead to certain denatured borrowings in contact situations, is also a way of playing with the meaning of normal and abnormal, norm and deviance. Because it occurs everywhere (however diverse its particular manifestations may be), it relativizes the incomparability of cultures and shows how cultures understood as ensembles of meaning relations are capable of adapting and of taking initiatives regardless of dominating contact situations. All societies attribute a status to deviants; all cultures recognize several forms of deviance and may even make use of deviance. At the individual level they all identify several forms of insanity, so that foreign groups, those whose customs the group in question does not want to reproduce, are never considered to be societies made up of crazy people in the same way as an individual can be crazy. Such foreigners are unquestionably barbarians, they may even be nonhuman, but they are not crazy people. As for the definition of the institutional deviant—the witch is an exemplary figure—it falls in between individual and collective conceptions of deviance. It is in this way that such deviance proves relative: the witch as a recognized and identified concrete individual may, in the most extreme circumstances, be excluded from society or put to death (this was not the case everywhere at all times), but witchcraft as relation is inherent to the social structure and it is indispensable to comprehending events, conceived as they are as effects of socially normed relations between individuals. Two other forms of deviance, which I willingly call normative (somewhat in the sense that the American ethnologist Ralph Linton used when he spoke of "models of misbehavior"), have to do on the one hand with ritual practices of inversion, on the other with how power is symbolized.

Rites of inversion have been studied attentively by ethnologists, and historians have analyzed phenomena of the same type.[7] We know that under certain circumstances the norms that a society usually respects are officially no longer respected, and in certain aspects may even seem inverted. This "inversion" affects essentially two types of social relations: those between men and women—men assume certain feminine roles and women certain masculine ones, with a complete reversal in some cases—and relations between ruler and ruled, as for example when a slave takes the place of the newly deceased king and mocks blood princes with impunity. Several types of inversion may also be combined. During smallpox epidemics in certain regions of the Togolese East, it was the custom to make offerings to Sakpakta, the smallpox god, of all the foods ordinarily forbidden him. According to one semihumorous exegesis, it was hoped the god would feel sick from all the forbidden food and take flight. The women in charge of this delicate operation were priestesses of the goddess Avlekete, whose natural referent is the foam of the waves (Avlekete is associated with running, bubbling waters as opposed to the calm depths of the sea). These women were called upon to break all prohibitions; their daily duty was to adopt patently masculine behavior, and during official ceremonies, dressed as men and complete with wooden phalluses, they would throw themselves into spectacular demonstrations.

Two remarks. First, manifestations of official inversion, at least in Africa, always take place in particular types of circumstances, either recurrent or accidental, which are the object of specific ritual treatment everywhere in the world: changes in season or social status (especially status connected with age), periods of interregnum, or in the advent of natural catastrophes such as epidemics. Second, the reversals that take place in these circumstances are in fact closer to a *perversion* of roles than a genuine inversion of them. Women *caricature* men at such moments, and vice-versa (during the circumcision ceremonies of the Wiko of Central Africa studied by Max Gluckman, for example).[8] In Ivory Coast an Agni slave would caricature the deceased king whose place he took for a time. During the ceremony of the first fruits among the Zulu, the warriors would sing their hatred of the king; as part of enthronement ceremonies, every new Yao chief was struck, thrown to the ground, and symbolically put to death. We have here a whole series of "borderline" ritualizations that, though they seem to underline rather than express rejection of the ensemble of culturally and socially instituted differences, also push them to the extreme of caricature and distribute them for a time in apparently deviant fashion, thereby conferring on them an eminently problematic character. It is always possible, from a functionalist perspective, to demonstrate the obvious point that these mechanisms only reinforce—indeed, that they aim to reinforce—the established order. But it is more interesting, it seems to me, to insist on the fact that the very logic of ritual involves explicitly underlining and consciously playing with and making use of the established character of the discriminations that constitute the social. To invert or pervert the discriminations that instate the social, to play on the borders of norm and deviance by reversing the positions, is both to postulate their necessity and to acknowledge their relative arbitrariness—in the same way as grammar exercises like the one Monsieur Jourdain receives from his philosophy tutor postulate at least the necessity of word order.[9]

The widely observed fact that inversion/perversion is possible constitutes a first element in the possible comparison of cultures, no doubt because it relativizes the definition of culture as an achieved totality. Regardless of the historical destiny of inversion rituals—and there is no reason to think they couldn't "go off the rails" one day, no reason that formal rebellion couldn't give rise to real rebellion—the important thing, it seems to me, is that such rituals, because they obey a syntax and because numerous cultures apparently find it necessary to use that syntax, constitute a limit to the culturalist reserve and identitary pride (*quant-à-soi*) of all societies.

Offical inversion/perversion naturally implies a certain number of transgressions of the usual norms; this is no doubt what accounts in certain cases for the need to use specialized personnel (the priestesses of Avlekete against smallpox, for example). But the instating of power often, and even by definition, involves transgressing these same norms; power's position is *necessarily* one of inversion/perversion. Power, it may be objected, obeys norms other than those that constitute the ordinary social order. This obvious point–that those who incarnate authority must be recognized and distinguished from all others–nonetheless does not, if we think about it, go without saying. Why should it be the case not only that the power in place obeys specific norms but that these norms are, in many instances, purely and simply the opposite or the reverse of those that direct the social order founded and legitimated by that power? Africa provides numerous examples of "royal incest"–the king marrying his agnate half-sister–and more complex formulas: in the Agni kingdom of the Sanwi, it was the king's sister or uterine cousin, the "queen mother" of Akan tradition, who gave birth to her brother's or cousin's successor; she enjoyed total sexual freedom. Examples of the king or other political-religious authorities (such as the lance-master among the Dinka) being put to death, willing their own death, or, conversely, of their death being denied for a prolonged period of time, show us that in matters of death and succession, as in those of alliance and reproduction, the royal person has a very particular status. Ever since Sir James Frazer and his analyses of the "divine king," anthropologists and sociologists (with Durkheim at the top of the list) have in a general way wondered about the significance of the greatly varied interdictions that weigh upon the sovereign. He may be forbidden to set a bare foot on the ground, to walk at anything other than a regular, stately pace, to bathe; these interdictions tend to immobilize or mineralize him, as it were. Ancient Mexico, Japan, and Africa offer quite comparable examples in this respect. In all of them the king, like the witch, stands as an instituted deviant in relation to purely social norms.

King and witch correspond to two complementary necessities that are tied to a certain image of individuality: the social must be thinkable, and power must be possible. The social is "thought" in terms of a logic of interdiction (whose fundamental, founding character Lévi-Strauss demonstrated in his study of incest), a logic that implies the possibility of transgression—incarnated by the imagined figure of the witch—as a means of accounting for disorder in events. Power is only possible if it escapes the system of relations whose necessity it guarantees, for if it were an integral part of that system this would relativize it. Power stands above and beyond the norm it institutes. Very simply, power *is*—at least this is how it means to present itself—like a necessity of nature, preceding the social that proceeds from it, founding and fundamental. In a way, the witch is an individual by default; he or she is identified only as an explanation of the misfires of the social relation (the local social code handles relations between mother and children, spouses, uncle and nephew, companions of the same age group, and so on). The king, on the other hand, is individual through excess: he escapes relation not so that he may explain its fortunes and misfortunes but rather so as to found its necessity. In extreme situations, an identified witch in certain regions of Africa could be put to death according to procedures aimed at excluding him from the cycle of reincarnation: it was necessary for him never to have existed. Conversely, the political or political-religious power in charge never dies: whether the king's real death was voluntary, denied, or marked by the sacrifices that accompanied it, it is only the occasion to reaffirm his singular lineage, wherein the permanence of the royal figure has shape and meaning. (All of this pertains, of course, only to *representations* of power; we must also be aware of the rivalries or *coups d'Etat* that marked the real life of African kingdoms, like any others.) In the contexts I have been elucidating, witch and king could be defined as two great abnormal beings charged with evacuating the very idea of deviance.

We sense therefore that the game played with norm and deviance within cultures that consider themselves closed totalities could very well define an intellectual totalitarianism, the same temptation to be all-powerful to which various sectarian and messianic movements have succumbed. These movements, it should be noted, arise in circumstances that rituals of inversion/perversion "normally" try to master: natural catastrophes and social or political crises. On the subject of millenarian movements from the eleventh to the sixteenth centuries, Norman Cohn has shown how symmetrical and opposed figures of good and evil settled into place, figures that have hardly disappeared in our time. He notes how the outbreaks of messianism that gave rise to these figures had many points in common–leaving aside differences in cultural context and scale–with the totalitarian movements of the twentieth century.[10] His demonstration is certainly valid today. But it must not be forgotten that, in their diverse but nonetheless comparable forms, what all these movements proceeded from was an intensification of the principles that constitute social life and power. Some of these applied to the reconciling of order and event, others to transcending both. From this point of view, contemporary prophetism in Africa is quite comparable to European millenarianisms.

Cultures differ, but we must not lose sight of the plastic and problematic character of every culture. With this in mind, let me propose a few ideas, and a few directions research could take.

First, a general remark. In recent years, now that God is dead, it has been considered good form to celebrate the death of Man. Whatever personal feelings each of us might have about the first of these deaths, the spectacle we are witnessing today seems to me to counsel a degree of circumspection. But what was meant by those who first proclaimed the death of Man? Once the measure of all things (Descartes's *cogito* as the extension of Protagoras's aphorism), Man had become an object of science; human reality was therefore divisible and recomposable according to the particular concerns and interests of each discipline. The fact that the object of human sciences was also its subject didn't make any difference because epistemology, psychology, cognitive disciplines in general, now took knowing, itself, as an object of knowledge. This existential pessimism proceeds from the observation that man is not God–or that as God he is dead–and its complement, that all objects of study are constructed, and, in the case of people, we can never thoroughly apprehend the singular reality of a single one of them but rather must proceed by way of groupings and abstractions, observing regularities, that is, norms, and disparities, departures from those norms. Finally, it proceeds from the rediscovery of the paradoxes and unfathomable complexities of reflective consciousness.

The procedure that I would like to sketch out here moves in the opposite direction; it involves, therefore, a reexamination of our notion of culture. Just as it has been written that savages are not chil-

dren because they *have* children (whom they recognize as such); just
as no culture can stand as the deviance or the madness of another
culture because that culture defines its *own* deviances and recognizes its own crazy people; so we cannot oppose the idea of culture
to that of singular individual identity, for each culture sets itself the
objective of defining individuality and determining identities. The
problematic character that we can recognize in every culture when
we look at it from the outside because we see the games it plays with
norm and deviance must also be detected *from within*, in its most
intimate manifestations. The best ethnological studies, those whose
authors have taken the time necessary to infuse the expression "participatory observation" with meaning, have shown the importance
within a given culture of ritual practices devoted to identifying every
singular person and to the reciprocal putting into perspective of
same and other. In societies that have not developed real scientific
theory, these practices are also aimed at conceiving and mastering
the relation between inert and living matters, nature and people,
people in the plural and "man" in the singular. The ethnological
study of rites has undoubtedly been influenced by the concern to
show either that rites serve in the functioning of a given society or
that they express and support a given state of society. But the majority of such rites, whether they be carried out on the occasions of
birth, adolescence, marriage, or death, an accident or an illness, involve singular matters whose importance and problematic character must not be masked over by the formal norms that simultaneously make the accomplishing of every rite a social act. An ethnology satisfied with recording the intelligent comments of a privileged
informer is of course vulnerable in some ways, but an ethnologist
who is not interested (and I say this because I believe in the value of
studies of form and structure) in the *content* of local requirements,
in the precise details of myths and rites, in the "propositional" and
not just "illocutory" value of the different types of utterances,
whether stereotypical or singular, which he or she is in a position to
collect and record runs the grave risk of developing an unconscious
and perverse form of ethnocentrism: that of attributing social mechanisms and determinism to "studied" societies and all reflection on
general and particular to the societies from which the "studiers"
come.

The best way to respect a contemporary culture, and to avoid considering it an arbitrary, closed ensemble of direct or indirect propositions, a "text," such as an archivist might discover, classify, or decipher, is to engage in dialogue with it, either metaphorically or not, depending on the circumstances. In other words, we must not renounce the affirmation of values judged universal in the name of a type of respect for cultures that is more like a form of cultural apartheid.

This reaffirming of values puts parameters into play that intervene in the definition of all cultures in the global sense of the term. Earlier, we contrasted the discriminating character of the social, which follows a logic of interdiction, and the unthinkable character of power with its logic of transgression. It is obvious that the democratic ideal involves, on the one hand, the least degree of social discrimination, and on the other, the socializing of power. The correlative of this is an idea of human individuality as liberated as possible from all appearance of "class" belonging in the logical sense of the term. Given that we cannot apply to cultures the equivalent of the declaration that every individual is equal to every other in rights and before the law, it is not precisely true to say that all cultures are of equal worth. Neither is it precisely true to say that modern Western culture is the finished model that answers perfectly to this demand for an ideal culture, or that it has long been the incarnation of individual rights. To realize this we need not even refer to the intellectual and human ravages of Nazism, but only to more common examples of segregation according to criteria of sex, age, origin, or sexual behavior. In order to understand that cultures are problematic and may evolve without being lost, I need only think of my grandparents' generation, or of Victor Margueritte's being dropped from the order of the Legion of Honor in 1923 for having written *La Garçonne*,[11] or of images representing the *âges de la vie* that can still be found in French attics and that assign in minimalist rhymes a place and role to each sex: of "woman" we may read, *A cinquante ans elle s'arrête. Au petit-fils elle fait fête* (At the age of fifty she stops everything; she celebrates her grandson); of "man," *A cinquante ans c'est l'âge mûr. Il pèse le passé, le futur* (Fifty is the age of maturity; he weighs past and future). Mores evolve, it is said, but it is rather cultural norms that move, the frontiers of deviance that change. It may seem obvious that positive development and, if we will, good deviances are those that enlarge the space of what is normal and restrict the space of what is normative (and of deviance). This statement nonetheless requires three qualifications.

First of all, culture arises from historical practices in which people are actively engaged. The history of this century in Europe and elsewhere attests to this. Any idea we may have of norms' being absolutely immobilized or blocked in place by cultural factors reflects a distorted conception of cultural reality. In this field as in others, moreover, regression is also possible, and there is no reason mechanically to link *la libération des moeurs*–an expression that deceptively seems to embrace freedom of individual consciousness–to technical-economic evolution. We have ocular proof that such evolution involves quite the opposite risk. Up against the harshness of modern society, some may be tempted to take refuge in that very "class" or "crutch" identity whose exclusivity Devereux saw as the sign of an impending collapse of individual identity: "If one is *nothing but* a Spartan, a capitalist, a proletarian, a Buddhist, one is next door to being nothing, and therefore to not being at all."[12] What's more, developments in means of communication, the media, the role of business companies, and what has been called the globalization of culture go hand in hand with the dissemination of images of what men and women are supposed to be–the body that's *truly* in shape, the life that's *truly* happy. These new norms have come into being beneath a mask of freedom, and I am not sure that even in the West we have really reached a "postmodern" age where norms and counternorms are regarded with the same distance and irony.

Finally, we must be conscious of two essential limits. If it is impossible to conceive of the individual without relation, that is, without the social (the absolute individual, God, is unthinkable), it is no less impossible to conceive of the social without a minimum of institutional authority to make it manageable. There is no break in the continuum that runs from singular identity to different types of collective identity, but in order for norm definitions not to be arbitrary, we must be able to read along that continuum in both directions. All cultures may be assessed with this yardstick. There is no cultural immunity.

5   Knowledge and Recognition: Anthropology's Meaning and End

$\mathbf{T}$o a social anthropologist, the question of the utility of knowledge is doubly perverse. First, there is something perverse in binary oppositions such as hard sciences/soft sciences, exact sciences/human sciences, natural sciences/social sciences, or pure sciences/applied sciences. These pairs do not fully overlap, and handled with more or less naiveté or guile they tend to suggest, paradoxically, that social sciences only escape being inexact by being applied (I'll come back to this). The second way in which the question is perverse concerns more fundamentally the meaning of the words "utility" and "knowledge." That meaning seems to be taken for granted in the formulation of the question, though the object and nature of anthropological knowledge (in this just like other kinds of knowledge) are in fact deeply and literally problematic, as is, a fortiori, its utility. If indeed anthropological knowledge has meaning and an end, these cannot be reduced to what other scientific approaches or nonscientific imperatives would like them to be, however legitimate such approaches and imperatives are in themselves.

The question of the application and utility of scientific knowledges (not to mention the legitimacy of using them) is of general interest, but it's a trick question, or, if you will, a question-within-a-question-within-a-question question not exhausted by the successive answers that can be made to it. Reducing the problem of the utility of knowledge to that of its possible applications always means, in the end, asking about the usefulness (meaning, end, consequences) of use itself, a question with resonances by turns technical, pragmatic, and ethical. Mathematics, physics, chemistry can be *used* to make rockets–but what's the *use* of going to the moon? Any end may be justified by another, and reason exhausts itself searching for the last end. In the end, what we can question is the value of explicit or implicit ends; we can contest the objective and general reality of the values attached to ends conceived as means to other ends. Sensing that these "ends-means" cannot be those of knowledge, we may be tempted to think, on the contrary, that knowledge has no end other than itself.

But let's stick for a moment to the question of application as it has been formulated in the field of social sciences and especially anthropology. That anthropological knowledge can be useful–to the colonizers, first of all, and then to economic developers, and thereby even to those who were colonized and to what we call "developing" nations–is a hypothesis that arises progressively from the conjunction of at least three factors, all historical but each referring to a different history. The first history is colonial history. We know that from the beginning British anthropology was anthropology applied to the problems raised by colonization, and this was also true for France, though in a less systematic and institutionalized way. Military men and administrators became interested, more or less felicitously, more or less intelligently, with those whom they considered themselves to be in charge of. In this case, the desire to know arose from a need to act. Without succumbing to the convenience of retrospective indictments, suffice it to say here that important anthropological work came out of the very practice of colonization. We could even affirm, were we not aware of the cynicism of such a statement, that one unquestionably positive consequence of colonization was the advancement of anthropological knowledge. The academic world has often preferred to read the situation in the opposite way, which enables it either to extol or to condemn the assistance that anthropological knowledge is thought to have given in the realization of the colonizers' projects.

The second history is the history of the discipline, more precisely of a concept: culture. As we know, this has always been central to anthropological thought. Whatever definition of it one may choose, culture is often the field assigned to anthropology from without. According to this idea, as we have said, an anthropologist's task is to recover and restore to the world the "style" of each culture and shed light on its "mystery." This conception of culture and anthropology explains why the place accorded to social anthropology in reports by economic development firms simultaneously reflects an overestimation of its capacities and an underestimation of its role. The clearest formulation of this ambiguous status consisted in making anthropology the discipline most likely to bring to light whatever might be "slowing down development"; the developers' assumption was that whatever it was constituted the specificity of the culture in question. Overestimation, in that it was up to anthropologists to explain the inexplicable; underestimation, in that someone outside their field was defining their research object, an object whose elucidation would advantage actions that, for their part, were not being subjected to any critical assessment.

The third history, which no doubt leads to more nuanced and complex formulations than the second, is that of technocratic thinking itself. A strange commotion was produced at the confluence of this history and that of the discipline. First, anthropologists (some of them) came up with the idea of applying to their own societies the particular way of looking they had reserved for distant cultures. And they discovered, in the United States first of all, a demand for this kind of work from decision-makers and heads of businesses, a new technical and functional demand addressed not only to anthropologists but to researchers such as linguists, with the intention of using their knowledge in the development of artificial intelligence and new kinds of software. Let me be perfectly clear here. I am not in the least suggesting that social anthropology can't shed valuable light on modes of life in business corporations, housing developments peripheral to the city,[1] or the problems that arise when people of different age groups and ethnic groups find themselves inhabiting the same space–though it is to be hoped that anthropology will not become denatured by this work, that anthropologists won't become, for example, experts or counselors on social relations. Anthropologists' collaboration in targeted interdisciplinary research has shown itself to be quite fruitful, for example, in modifying certain established ideas in the fields of medicine and epidemiology. Serious ethnographic studies of Chinese, Tunisian, and Eskimo populations, for example, have helped bring to light the role played by nutritional factors associated with the Epstein-Barr virus in cancer of the rhinopharynx.

But no matter how useful the anthropological approach may be in the search for solutions to certain contemporary problems, the global utility of anthropological knowledge cannot be reduced to the possibility of its episodic collaboration with other disciplines in the interest of solving problems or formulating them better. It would be infinitely dangerous to reduce a discipline to the sum of finalized procedures it authorizes; we would be killing the goose that lays the golden eggs, sterilizing the discipline by being interested in some of its possible consequences and not others. This observation extends to the whole of anthropology's specified or "sectored" interventions, which anthropologists are sometimes too ready to constitute into autonomous disciplines or subdisciplines: medical anthropology, urban anthropology, legal anthropology, historical anthropology, and so forth. Here again, the pair overestimation/underestimation is applicable to anthropology's undertakings. Considered in some contexts an imperialist science, in others it becomes an auxiliary one. It is one thing for anthropological methods to be applied to extremely diverse areas, including those that other sciences hold to be their principal objects of study; it is quite another for each one of these applications to engender its own discipline. And it would be a serious mistake, to my mind, to reduce the utility of anthropological knowledge to the help such sub-anthropologies can provide in the analysis of objects constituted and defined by other sciences.

We come back to our initial observation: asking what use can be made of knowledge is not a good way of asking about knowledge's usefulness. Applied to anthropology, this question has elicited plenty of partial responses that correspond to as many finalized, mutilating, and in some cases unjust definitions. Everything can be used to all ends (war *and* peace, exploitation *and* emancipation); that much is obvious. Should we for all that proclaim the uselessness of knowledge, and more particularly of anthropological knowledge, of which we would then postulate that it has no end other than itself?

Let it be said right away that such an affirmation does not elimi-

nate the problem of knowledge's object but rather tends to acknowledge that it is indissociable from the problem of knowledge as
object-of-knowledge. In this sense there is no science without consciousness: consciousness of the fact that man in his biological, neu-
ronal, psychological, and sociological reality is part of what he
means to know. Regardless of the object he turns to, the effort to
know entails ipso facto a better knowledge of man by man, a better
knowledge of knowledge itself, and of man as subject and object of
knowledge. Montaigne used his partaking of the "human condition" to legitimate his project of showing other human beings what
he believed he knew of himself. But the human condition, whose
"shimmering and various character" Montaigne recorded with
skeptical curiosity, is not to be separated either from the world of
which it is a part or the nature from which it arises. Man's necessary
relation with the world was characterized by Heidegger with the formula *in der Welt sein*, "being in the world." Milan Kundera evokes
this formula in his *Art of the Novel* to suggest that the novel, whose
sole *raison d'être* is "to say what only the novel can say," has since
Balzac examined "the historical dimension of human existence":
"Man and the world are bound together like the snail to its shell: the
world is part of man, it is his dimension, and as the world changes,
existence (*in der Welt sein*) changes as well. Since Balzac, the world
of our being has a historical nature, and characters' lives unfold in a
realm of time marked by dates."[2] But man as a historical being is
nonetheless a being of and in nature, and the same intuition that le-
gitimates Montaigne's project and the Heideggerian definition of
man nourished, it seems to me, Freud's scientific optimism when,
at the end of *The Future of an Illusion*, he wrote:

> An attempt has been made to discredit scientific endeavor in a radical
> way, on the ground that, being bound to the conditions of our own
> organization, it can yield nothing else than subjective results, whilst
> the real nature of things outside ourselves remains inaccessible. But
> this is to disregard several factors which are of decisive importance
> for the understanding of scientific work. In the first place, our orga-
> nization–that is our mental apparatus–has been developed precisely
> in the attempt to explore the external world, and it must therefore
> have realized in its structure some degree of expediency; in the sec-
> ond place it is itself a constituent part of the world which we set out to
> investigate, and it readily admits of such an investigation.[3]

Here anthropology regains its rights, or at least its place, since a human being, whose every act of knowing presupposes his or her existence as both subject and object, is a plural being. Every individual exists in and through his or her relation to others, and people differ from each other in gender, character, ethnocultural belonging, social position, and so forth. Concretely, man as object (and subject) of knowledge can only be known through two conjoined modes, those of same and other, and it is the play of this double modality that is anthropology's object, above and beyond the diversity of its empirical fields of observation.

Qualified at times in terms of this cognitive aspect, anthropology studies the procedures by which human societies have undertaken to master the world intellectually and practically. We must observe of these procedures–the elaboration of local anthropologies, pantheons, various taxonomies–first, that their effect has been to organize people's lives around the assumption of, and in relation and accordance with, a measurable, masterable universe, and their utility has been to keep the species alive; second, that they postulate that same indissociability of man and world as objects of knowledge that seems to me the very principle of the act of knowing. But becoming conscious of–*knowing*–these procedures necessarily means measuring the intellectual and practical risks inherent in them, and anthropology has the virtue of being able to identify these risks. I would say that this is the first of its merits, its primary utility, for, far from being exclusive to societies where the anthropologist may flush them out with ease, such risks threaten every society and all individuals of a given society. I am referring to the risks of *reconnaissance* (recognition). Those of *méconnaissance* (mis-knowing) are only a possible consequence of these.

No society exists that has not tried to master intellectually the world in which it has its place by constructing, for its own "personal" use, images of man, of interhuman relations, of nature, and of relations between man and nature. But the temptation to do so results less, it seems to me, from a desire to know (*connaître*) than a need for meaning, a need to recognize oneself in the world (*s'y reconnaître*). By a short-circuiting of thought everywhere attested, people desire less to know the world than to recognize themselves in it, substituting for the indefinite frontiers of an ungraspable universe the totalitarian security of closed worlds.

Three remarks to nuance or clarify this affirmation. When I speak of the totalitarianism of societies traditionally studied by ethnologists, I am referring to the systematic will for totalization attested to by specialists in interpretation and diagnosis. This is intellectual totalitarianism, or rather holism, but a holism from whose practical consequences no individual is exempt. To interpret is to translate an event belonging to what seems to us a clearly determined field (psychology, for example) into the language of another (that of intrafamilial relations, for example). No gesture can be made, no word pronounced that is not susceptible of turning against its author the moment another interpretation requires interpreting. In these types of interpretation–African lineage-based societies provide a good example–it is always impossible to be mistaken: as explained in Chapter 4, any new element can only lead to a reformulation of the diagnosis, never to its invalidation. Likewise the death of a sick person is never the fault of the one giving him or her therapy. The totalizing effect suffices to turn any "error" into a partial or temporary truth. It is also strong enough to explain all types of passivity: the passivity of the Tupinamba prisoners in the Amazon, whom I mentioned in Chapter 1, as well as that of the slave who played the king's double in the Agni kingdom of the Sanwi, a man who knew that he was not to survive the death of his master and likeness.

The totalitarian character of the interpretive grid is not, however, a product of absolute arbitrariness. The same societies that have elaborated cosmogonies, cosmologies, anthropologies, and pantheons have also cultivated nature, established norms of collective life, insured the production of goods and the reproduction of human beings. Their control over nature is effective. Western or Christian eyes try to distinguish in these societies what is a matter of rational empiricist activity and what has more to do with a withdrawal into the irrational; the societies themselves do not effect this split, and the field (to borrow a term from modern sociology) in which they are intellectually active is, in their eyes, homogeneous. The rites that accompany seed-planting are not a ceremonial luxury; no more is it a paradox that witchcraft scenarios or, more generally, struggles for influence between social actors, correspond to real tensions and finely observed psychological realities. It should be added that for these societies themselves, the ideal of totalization (and, we might add, of totalitarian security) is only that, an ideal: their history is often one of incessant moving and displacement, migrations, temporary settlements, lost wars. To effect a symbolic quartering-off of space, to become once again the center of the earth, is also to stop moving and settle down: behind these closed ideological systems is the memory of more or less disordered errancy, just as behind the ritual activity that marks and accompanies the cyclical regularity of the seasons is fear of climatic disorders. Through the multiplicity of their spatial and temporal landmarks, we may say that such ideologies of recognition result from experience and constitute a kind of knowledge (*savoir*).

But this knowledge is only meaningful within the frontiers it has built around itself, inside what I propose to call a universe of recognition. And it must be added (my third remark) that the profound seduction of closure that makes people constitute such universes is not reserved to lineage-based or primitive societies. We experience its effects daily. Any community of work, leisure, or opinion tends to constitute itself as a universe of recognition, and we may consider with amused sympathy the more or less secret understandings and feelings of fellowship that unite the members of this or that vacation club for the space of a week, office colleagues or sports fans in a more regular way. But the ideal of recognition can function in a sociologically more meaningful way. The loyalty to a particular political party or religion expressed by those who no longer follow unreservedly its credo; class culture; nationalisms more or less colored by xenophobia or racism—all these also involve systems of recognition. Once again, the situations are not completely fixed, first because a single individual can recognize himself or herself, even contradictorily if need be, in several universes of recognition; second because some universes are less closed than others: closure is only a risk or virtuality for them. Some politicians are aware of this, and readily accuse their opponents of practicing *la politique politicienne* or *la langue de bois* so as to differentiate themselves from them.[4] But this type of denunciation can itself become a sign of recognition. In a more general way, it is interesting to observe that the ideology of economic liberalism tends to make the business firm into a universe of recognition where the feeling of belonging is supposed at all levels of the hierarchy to be stronger than any feelings of difference or conflicts of interest. Virtually totalitarian, the "true" spirit of enterprise–as we have seen in Japan–overflows the limits of the workplace, marking and ordering employees' daily routines and even their vacations, which are organized, like everything else, by the employer.

In universes of recognition one willingly speaks the language of relativism. The trite expressions of ordinary relativism–"there's no accounting for taste," *"à chacun sa vérité"* (to each his truth), *"tous les goûts sont dans la nature"* (there is no appetite or desire that cannot be found in human nature)–express something quite the opposite of tolerance. Their real purpose and effect is to legitimate those who utter them, exclude others, and close down discussion, because what is particular about such universes is that despite their closure they think of themselves as being universal and *they don't recognize each other* (in the same way that one political state may refuse to recognize another). Indeed, they can only exist in a state of mutual *méconaissance* (ignorance and misappreciation). During a march organized in April 1987 in Marseille by Mr. Le Pen's extreme right National Front party, some of the people who were loudly proclaiming that France must continue to belong to the French, that being French is something one has to deserve, abandoned themselves to a remarkable surge of nostalgia and began chanting "Algérie française!" Newspapers picked up the apparent contradiction without really being surprised by it: the coexistence of these slogans is only contradictory *outside* the universe in which Mr. Le Pen's followers recognize themselves.

Ordinary relativism is essentially defensive, corresponding to a refusal to recognize oneself in the other and thereby deal a blow to the reassuring feeling of identity. What we find most difficult to bear (I say "we" because we all belong to universes of recognition) is the mirror handed to us by another in which we see the spectacle of our own image. The extravagance of a tyrant like Bokassa shocked Europe, especially France, all the more keenly in that it was in no way foreign: the opulence of his enthronement ceremonies seemed less like an exotic invention than like what we might see in a magnifying mirror.[5]

The different "universes" I have been referring to are not, of course, sociologically equivalent, but they are epistemologically comparable in that they all constitute units productive of discourse and interpretation. Still, they are only virtually homogeneous, and it

is clear that from a sociological point of view they are also characterized by internal differences and particular situations; these include some of the things to which we refer when we speak of the "culture" of a given ethnic group or the "ideology" of a dominant class.
I have just suggested that the only relation obtaining between universes of recognition is mutual nonrecognition; indeed, this is what
justifies the use of the term "universe." The same can be said for the
relations obtaining between activities of knowledge and activities of
recognition. While seeming to pursue the same *objective* (healing,
for example), they do not set themselves the same *object*, and it is
surely one of anthropology's strongest strong points to be able to
identify the effects of totalization and circularity that radically distinguish the second from the first–though we cannot exclude the
possibility that activities of knowledge (scientific research) can at
moments, and sometimes at length, fall into the trap of recognition
effects, where, fascinated by fixed paradigms, they stubbornly re-
peat the rediscovery of America.

Let me come back for a moment to a theme and a region that I
have discussed at length elsewhere. These remain, it seems to me,
a useful example of the specific effects induced by the mutual inter-
ference or scrambling of procedures of knowing and recognition. I
have been working for some years in Ivory Coast with personages
who call themselves "prophets" and who simultaneously fulfill therapeutic, religious, economic, and, in a broad sense, political functions–political to the extent that their action stands in a precise relation to the government policy of economic development. The
prophets are first and foremost healers. They have a thorough
knowledge of the surroundings, vegetation, and resources of the villages in which they have settled, and have effected that symbolic
quartering of nature by means of which all cultural identities affirm
themselves. Whatever *they* may say about it–for, recreating the
world, they seek to be recognized as holders of *new* knowledge–
their knowledge is in this sense "traditional," just like that of healers who don't claim to be prophets. Likewise, their schemata for interpreting illness hearken back to models that are well known to
those who come to consult them: aggression through witchcraft,
curses, and transgression of interdictions constitute their principal
etiological models. Illness and ill-fortune are for them profoundly

similar types of problems, but this is not new either. What is new is the nature of the misfortunes they deal with, for to traditional troubles have been added those of modern times: failure in school, professional difficulties, unemployment. Those who come to consult are victims of the cruelties of lineage-based village life, but also of the harshness of urban life. Furthermore, as the prophets' audiences grow and they become known, their clienteles become more and more ethnically diverse. Those with such a following are beginning to be a problem for the authorities, less because of the content of their message (which never contradicts official policy) than because of the large crowds gathering around them, a fact that underlines without the prophets having tried to that all is not for the best in the best of all possible worlds.

The communities that form around them adopt under their direction a way of life, a schedule, and ritual practices that are organized in relation to what I have called a universe of recognition. A prophet generally will not utter a word about those who also lay claim to that title; he pretends to ignore them. It very often happens that his former patients stay close to him, even though they say they have been cured, and start working for him—which clearly shows that they came for something more than just a cure. Conversely, every prophet is haunted by the fear that a disappointed patient will leave him for another—no vain worry, for on questioning the patients one realizes they have "tried out" a great number of "therapists," this term referring to practitioners of Western medicine in rural community clinics or urban hospitals as well as healers and prophets of all denominations.

In comparison to ritual practice as analyzed above, prophetic practice is by definition unbalanced. Those who come to the prophets have no fixed place either in village or city; they are having trouble situating themselves on the axis of identity. It's their belonging that is in question: they belong neither here nor there; their position cannot be expressed in terms of sum total and ambivalence. The ambiguity thus substituted for ambivalence on the identity axis is resolved by focusing on the person of the prophet, and since he cannot tell them that they come from nowhere, he suggests to them that their place is with him. Meanwhile, on the axis of relation and otherness, ambivalence is substituted for ambiguity: the prophetic

88   KNOWLEDGE AND RECOGNITION

message has a hard time conjugating the relations of same and other from the moment it encounters the colonial situation or the globalizing of stakes. "In seven years, Blacks will be like Whites," was what Harris, a renowned Ivory Coast prophet active early in the century, used to say, speaking the language of deferred ambivalence: "You shall be black *and* white, but later." And when, today, people come to the prophets with their difficulties and the prophets in reply lash out against the lying ways or bad witchcraft of their faithful, whom they present as the cause of both their own particular problems and a situation judged to be on the whole disastrous, it sometimes happens that, because they cannot claim an alienated ambivalence (they are *not* Blacks who have become Whites), they reduce to à single quality–that of being Black–and a single cause–the Black's insufficiency–a state of affairs that can no longer be put into relation with any other. The masochistic tone audible at times in the prophetic message (which, in another context, could be heard as racist) testifies to a difficulty in symbolizing ties that have been broken and not redefined. The kind of house arrest that a prophet-healer, concerned to keep his patients or faithful close to him in the insularity of his fragile utopia, tries to formulate corresponds to a disturbance of ritual language, a disturbance tied to the difficulty of mediating between incommensurable worlds.

Of what nature, then, is the prophets' knowledge? What can I as an anthropologist know of these personages and the institutions they operate? And what could the meaning and end of such knowledge be? To try to answer these questions, it is first of all necessary to note the questions addressed *to* the anthropologist, as much by the prophets themselves as by some of those who, doctors or not, have heard about them. All the prophets I'm discussing would like to collaborate with medical practitioners and the hospital institution, and to be recognized as collaborators by the government authorities. It is also true that certain people with political or medical responsibilities are interested in the possibility of associating what are called traditional practitioners with official medicine.

What anthropology reveals to us is precisely the impossibility of such collaboration. The prophets are not primarily interested in illness as such; they can only identify if need be certain symptoms of illness, and these are not necessarily determinant in formulating a diagnosis and prescribing therapy. As for taking the sick person's global context into consideration, which is the only way the prophets can recognize a known situation, formulate hypotheses, and test treatments—as one may guess, this does not constitute a valuable addition to physical treatment. Once he has carried out his act of clairvoyance, the prophet attacks the whole of a given situation, and he needs to be able to use persuasion on the supposed aggressor as well as to exercise vigilance over the sick victim in order to correct what are for him perturbed relations and compromised balances. (The notions of relation and balance apply here simultaneously to fields that we distinguish from each other even as we associate them—social, corporal, psychic; the prophets, heirs in this sense to the pagan tradition, conceive of them as continuous.) It would therefore be a grave mistake to think that the prophet's word or practice would point up *the* psychological or sociological element that would, were it taken into consideration, help a practitioner of standard medicine. Not that the prophet doesn't hear the patient's demand; often he hears that demand more completely than the doctor, because prophet and patient have the same frame of reference and the prophet recognizes himself in the patient's complaint just as the patient does in the prophet's diagnosis. But this recognition effect cannot be decomposed. Prophets are not concerned to be more "humane" toward their patients than the doctor is; indeed, they are often harsher with them. If someone is sent to a prophet because that person is believed crazy, the first thing the prophet might do is chain him up. And prophets don't take the social context into consideration in order to improve the cure; from their point of view that cure is being applied to a being substantially defined by his or her relation to others. In this way the paradigm from which prophets work resembles more closely that of behavioral psychotherapists or psychologists than that of bio-medicine. It would be wrong, however, to believe that prophets are concerned with psychology; in such matters they have no advice to give whatsoever. They want to be admitted to work in the hospital so as to cure as doctors do, or even perhaps in order to invalidate their diagnoses, not to serve as their interpreters, public relations advisors, psychologists, or ethnographers. The clearest evidence of this is that when the prophet himself sends patients to the hospital they are generally what he deems hopeless cases who have reached him too late, not patients whom he has begun to treat and for whom he requires a complementary treatment.

Any idea of a possible collaboration between prophet-healers and doctors is a delusion, despite past or present experiments, because it could only arise from a fundamental misunderstanding. The knowledge and practice of anthropology, on the other hand, *can* be useful to doctors, regardless of the society in which they practice, precisely because medicine as a practical healing activity involves observing and recognizing clinical signs. Decoding patients' demands could only improve and enrich diagnoses.

Obviously not all anthropologists are doctors, and social anthropology does not study the facts of illness in any exclusive way. What the example of the Ivory Coast prophets more fundamentally teaches, I believe, and what I have privileged here, is that social anthropology constitutes critical knowledge. I have tried to suggest that social anthropology is above all an effort to *know* the effects of recognition, which are antinomic to all procedures of genuine knowing. Three clarifications are necessary in this connection. The first and second I have already formulated: recognition effects are not exclusive to given types of society, and every procedure aimed at acquiring knowledge can bring about effects of recognition that block cognitive progress.

My third remark concerns universes of recognition themselves. They do not arise either out of the irrational or from an incapacity to conceptualize, but rather from an ideal of intellectual security whose necessary and salutary character in certain historical circumstances may be readily understood. It is nonetheless true that the desire-to-know must take measures to protect itself from the need-to-recognize-everything that subverts it. Like common sense for Descartes, the need to recognize is probably the most common human need. And it readily makes itself felt in the area of study that social anthropology has chosen for itself; namely, instituted relations between individuals, definitions of same and other, relations between individual identity and collective identity such as they are elaborated, reproduced, and modified throughout societies existing historically in all their diversity. Which is to say that in contrast to the prosifying Monsieur Jourdain, plenty of people claim to know about anthropology without having done any.[6] I cited above a few of the trite maxims of ordinary relativism ("to each his truth," for example), more redolent of apartheid than tolerance. They are among those "obvious things" or recognition effects that tend to impose themselves as natural in certain groups during certain periods. Political discourse, media images, advertising messages all take the tone of someone who's stating the obvious, and in this they are all related to anthropological observation. Anthropological observation, however, has the formidable privilege of being able to apply its techniques to the very institutions and messages that assign themselves more or less the same object as anthropology. It's an old habit: anthropology is always the study of others' anthropology, and others think and have always thought something about the relations between individuals and groups, between same and other. They do not stop at thinking something about it, but have put that something into operation, and it is this "acting out" that social anthropology is interested in when it studies matrimonial systems, the instituting of the political, or modes of production and goods circulation.

The knowledge social anthropology elaborates can thus be evaluated from two points of view: in relation to the internal logic of the systems it apprehends, and in relation to the knowledge that those who do not have an anthropological knowledge of these systems have or think they have. I have insisted, in the case of the Ivory Coast prophets, on the deductive and repetitive character of the diagnoses authorized by a grid of interpretation that always situates the patient and the people close to him or her within a certain number of typical scenarios. But apprehended from without, the prophetic system could well be *misknown* because too quickly *recognized* as irrational (from the point of view of logic), subversive (from a political point of view), or inoperative (from a medical point of view). Conversely, it can happen that what an external observer remarks, just as arbitrarily, is the prophetic institution's therapeutic effectiveness and social and economic exemplarity. The real teaching of anthropology in this is both more modest and surer. First, it can demonstrate the relative intellectual coherence of the models of interpretation used and show how that coherence, which characterizes how social structure, interindividual relations, and organic balance are brought into relation, is more readily operative in a relatively stable social state than in the present situation, where the urban environment and the larger global context impose trials which lineage structure can no longer account for. The prophets perceive this difficulty (this is why they are prophets and not merely healers) and can only proceed by becoming social inventors or innovators. If it is true that many of their former patients stay with them (while patients who are not cured leave them), this is because the prophets offer them a new type of community, neither traditional or modern; more exactly, neither that of the village in the traditional sense of the term or the city. The prophet seeks the impossible: the reconciliation in his person of the demands of modern development with the ancient ways of meaning—but we should note that this will is itself an element of African modernity. And it is in this that such will is of interest to the anthropologist: by the challenge it addresses and the problem it poses to political actors, economic developers, and administrators, who must accept becoming themselves objects of anthropological scrutiny. Anthropology's gaze must not identify itself with *their* preoccupations (and this is, to my mind, anthropology's second message) even though these are of interest to it, but must rather, refusing to recognize itself in them, seek to know them. As an anthropologist, my study of the prophetic institution embraces all that is not that institution but is necessarily related to it: politicians, doctors, all those in relation to whom the prophet claims to situate himself and who are themselves seeking to place the prophet. The game of same and other by means of which each tries to include or engulf the other in a single recognition, each seeking the other's recognition, is played in both directions, and it is this double play that interests anthropologists—without their being able to recognize themselves in either of the two, or needing to.

It is the same in any situation of "development" or "modernization." As an object of anthropological scrutiny, an object of knowledge, this type of situation includes both the developers and the developees, the modernizers and those whose behaviors they intend to modernize, and most of all the ensemble of reciprocal relations that the first group has with the second, both on the level of fact and on the level of representation and imagination.

The "efficiency" brandished by those who proclaim the utility of science comes to have full meaning inside a universe of recognition whose parameters are both technical criteria and ethical values. And it is just this universe, in its entirety and global nature, which is the object of the anthropological gaze. To situate anthropology in this way *outside* the field where its utility is questioned is not to affirm its gratuitousness or make it a pure mind game, but rather to define a level of knowledge from which one may examine without complacency the effects of recognition and mis-knowing. In this connection the affirmation that sciences of European origin have condemned man to alienate himself through the very techniques by means of which he undertakes to explore the world seems more an expression than a condemnation of the ideology it intends to denounce. This is surely the place and moment to call to mind Lévi-Strauss's argument that the symbolic precedes any effort to know. For if there is one thing that societies concretely studied by ethnology display at all latitudes of the globe, it is the co-presence of the other at all levels of identity. The individual person is anchored in ancestors; lineage grouping depends on marital alliance; modern nations are haunted by the great Other–colonizer, developer, Christian God or Great Satan. These societies are proof on the one hand that alienation is always with us and is always with every one of us; on the other, that alienation is never self-evident. From this point of view, the alienation due to technology–the idea that products of knowledge are the cause of alienation–which is supposed to characterize the modern West is only one particular figure of the institutional alienation of which Castoriadis spoke in the 1960s. As such, it is just as problematic, and it deserves to be looked at by anthropologists whose gaze is not identifiable with that of the great Other–colonizer, developer, or technocrat–or a will to reduce all to the same. The tension particular to lineage-based societies, to situations of underdevelopment and prophetic discourse, is a tension that anthropologists are discovering at the heart of the Western world. This is the price to pay–the price of critical knowledge (*savoir*)–if anthropological knowledge is to maintain itself as knowledge and continue to refuse all confusing of ideologies with knowledge, without for all that proclaiming either that ideology is dead or that knowledge is useless.

6   The Conquest of Space

Excellent collective works written a few years back show
how the ethnological study of France freed itself from the folkloristic *études* it had been producing and the rural fieldwork it had at first
confined itself to. These works contributed more or less explicitly
to reformulating the fundamental question, what is anthropology?
or rather, what is its object? Anticipating a part of the answer, we
may say that this is in fact a version of the same question we have
been asking all along: Who is the other?

The question is polymorphous and is best answered in stages.
First, let me point out that ethnographic study of France, following
the path laid out by the Durkheimian school, developed in opposition to the folklorist tradition by *localizing* research and envisaging
its object as a *totality*.[1] The two precursors of this development most
regularly cited are Robert Hertz, whose "Saint-Besse, étude d'un
culte alpestre" (the results of an investigation conducted in the Val
d'Aoste in 1912) was published in 1928,[2] and Marcel Mauss, who con-
tinued teaching until 1939. Hertz took into account all aspects of the
phenomenon under study, from ritual to iconography, as well as all
groups concerned in one way or another by the given worship practices. Marcel Mauss accorded special value to the notion of totality
and underlined the importance of social morphology and technical
systems.

The reactualization of ethnographic research may be most fully appreciated in terms of its opposition to folklorist ethnography. With their *passé*-ist vision of society, French folklorists had privileged the study of traditional themes whose circulation they examined or whose disappearance they observed without being at all interested in how they were sociologically anchored–that is, without concerning themselves with the localized totalities that would become ethnography's specific object. While we can make more or less nuanced judgments of the folklorists (authors such as Arnold Van Gennep and André Varagnac were clearly sensitive to certain aspects of the ethnographic "totality"), the fact remains that ethnography's triumph consists in its conquest of space, its anchoring itself in place. From this point of view, and in the eyes of many contemporary observers, the publication of Louis Dumont's *La Tarasque* in 1951 marked the true birth of the modern anthropological study of France.[3]

As Christian Bromberger has explained it, this type of anthropology may be practiced from two distinct perspectives, which correspond to two scales of observation:

> The ethnologist who studies France these days often defines himself–or herself–as someone who works in a small field and perhaps on a small theme. But what small field? Some focus the microscope on the infinitely small; others seek to understand how the field functions, using astronomer's instruments to look out from their observation post; this depends on whether the field is considered the object, or simply the framework, of the research. In the first case we may speak of a monographic study, a local approach; in the second of a localized approach.[4]

These two options have indeed been operative in the ethnological research on France carried out in the last thirty or forty years. A number of studies that clearly followed Mauss, together with community studies done in Great Britain and the United States, privileged an approach that may be characterized as totalizing-monographic and whose ideal object was the *commune*, both village and administrative subdivision.[5] There seemed at first no opposition between a Marxist vision that brings into play all social elements and actors (in 1947 the reknowned Marxist historian Albert Soboul drew up a "research outline for a monograph of rural community")[6] and a functionalist conception of cultural totality. The work of Lucien

Bernot and René Blancard,[7] Laurence Wylie,[8] and their successors up until the present time may be inscribed in this perspective (Georges Ravis-Giordani's work on Corsican shepherds, for example, has involved attentive observation of village communities).[9]

Other research currents correspond to what Christian Bromberger calls "localized." Starting with local occurrences, they work to discover and expose general forms, systems analogous to those of language. In studies of institutions such as parallel kinship[10] or of codified practices such as the boar hunt,[11] ethnologists have worked first to understand the intimate meaning of the practice in question—one in which power relations (*rapports de force*) and meaning relations (*rapports de sens*) are expressed simultaneously; then to reconstitute the internal coherence of representations and make explicit the logical connections uniting apparently disparate manifestations. As analyzed by Daniel Fabre, this type of research begins with extremely localized observations (Jeanne Favret-Saada's work—see Complementary Sources—could stand as a paradigm, though its purpose is more pragmatic); then, taking care not to dissociate the study of symbolism from that of social elements and their organization, it points up the underlying logic in terms of which apparently arbitrary and disparate facts become meaningful.

It is not my purpose here to tell the story of how ethnology of the proximal, inspired by models for studying the remote (notably English and American models), conquered its territory, mastered its space, and planted its feet firmly on the ground. I would like instead to underline the two-sided and relatively paradoxical observation that can be made today about that history. While the ethnological study of France was trying to catch up with its exotic model, and at the very moment it was congratulating itself on its newfound dignity (Martine Segalen in *L'Autre et le Semblable* expresses her satisfaction at seeing ethnologists of the proximal be able to speak as equals with those of the remote),[12] a few ethnologists, marginal at first, noticed new objects coming into view, and it gradually became clear that these were situated in a different space-time. Leaning a bit hard on the words, we could say that in proximal ethnology, the localized approach triumphed at the very moment that "locales" began to disappear.

But places are like the social in general: they only disappear so as

to reshape themselves. More broadly speaking, it is the relations between space and otherness that should be addressed and analyzed
today if we are to point up some of the contradictions of our modernity. No sooner does Europe raise once again the issue of national
borders, no sooner do national identities begin to reaffirm themselves, than the notion of minority reappears, inevitable from the
moment that a nation is defined in relation to a majority ethnic
group but is also intended to conserve the space history has be-
queathed it. This is a strange turnabout for an Africanist ethnologist accustomed until now to seeing the media reduce the problem
of nationality to an ethnic question *only* in analyses of the countries
he studies. In Europe, or at least in that confirmed center of it that
makes up the European Community, the question of the place and
role of foreigners–immigrants–is being asked with insistence, and
quite naturally in spatial terms, by the extreme right, which, in its
particular version of the right to be different, postulates that foreigners have a right to respect so long as they stay home. The question is in fact posed in the same terms by those who, on the contrary,
are anxious for integration to take place and deplore the fact that in
some neighborhoods immigrant populations are grouped together
and become the majority. "Circulation," "wall," "ghetto," "sub-
urb,"[13] "border"–the vocabulary used today is indeed spatial, but
the words all have to do with the relation between same and other.

We can attempt to shed some light on the issue of space by taking
into account that of otherness, and vice-versa. This involves analyzing two spatial realities that stand in a relation of contrast and complementarity: place–which I have called anthropological place because the identity, relations, and history of those who inhabit it are
inscribed in its space–and non-place, by which I mean spaces of circulation, distribution, and communication where neither identity,
relation, or history may be apprehended.[14] Non-places are specific
to our age.

Anthropological space is defined first of all as *chez soi*, the place
of shared identity common to those who, inhabiting it together, are
identified as being *chez eux*, "at home," by those who do not inhabit
it. It must immediately be added that such a place fits ethnologists'
requirements and expectations so well that there is a permanent
danger that, taking their desire for reality, they will exaggerate the

homogeneity of the population under study and invent, at least in part, a kind of transparency in which society, culture, ethnic group, and individual are all identifiable with each other. This in turn will seem to legitimate their attempt to read the organization of a precisely circumscribed space as the form taken by the social organization, cultural and ethnic traits, and type of individual found there. Ethnologists have sometimes worked as if their goal was to take an inventory of what they somehow imagine as the complete set of insulated cultural groups inscribed in the space of the world; only after doing so do they begin worrying about the phenomena of circulation that are likely to connect these groups, put them into meaningful contact with one another, and affect their supposed original purity.

This temptation has never entirely disappeared, for a number of complementary reasons. First of all, ethnologists work in contemporary space. It's not that they want or are somehow obliged to ignore history, but their field is necessarily *present* space, and their first task is to take note of or carve out signifying units of that space, units that are thus conceived of from the beginning as corresponding to a certain identity that, more often than not, is summed up by the name of an ethnic group. Then there is the method—more or less distanced or participatory observation, interviews with privileged interlocutors—which has the ethnologist collecting varied information from the tongues of individuals who believe in the relevance for their own lives of all that they mention, describe, or explain to the ethnologist. This in turn explains the ethnologist's particular sensitivity to echoes and resonances between what may seem otherwise distinct categories—social, cultural, and individual—and a tendency to take the individual for a mere expression of, the social for the mere consequence of, a culture that the symbolized space of the ethnic territory condenses and materializes.

The culturalist temptation, particularly strong among American ethnologists, was already present in the work of Marcel Mauss, and its pull is felt in—and, it seems to me, propagated by—the works of Clifford Geertz. Culturalist tendencies are strongly suggested by the presence in ethnological writing of two elements: the metaphor of reading, which suggests both that a culture can be read and that such reading entails deciphering a given social reality and individual behaviors; and the use of the definite article, which, preceding the ethnic name in the singular, suggests the immutable nature of ethnic character as incarnated in its different individual expressions (and in spite of them). The Bambara, the Dogon, "the Melanesian of this or that island" dear to Marcel Mauss, are thus essentially—in the philosophic sense of that word—defined by the cultures of which each is conceived to be the undifferentiated expression.

We can easily see the dangers of a culturalist approach to societies. Not only does such an approach unduly substantialize and fix notions, distracting attention from the problematic, unstable, dialectical aspects of culture, the internal differences and tensions of the social, the unstable, relational, dynamic character of the individual personality; it also privileges a terminology whose lay use, even when it means to be moral, may lead to a segregationist vision of the world or of complex societies. Respect for differences, the idea of the right to be different, the notion of a "multicultural" society—all these, while generating noble-sounding expressions, may actually furnish an alibi to a ghetto ideology, an ideology of exclusion.

But this does not imply that ethnologists do not have good reasons to be interested in the relations between culture, society, and the individual, nor that they are wrong to analyze whatever is visible of these relations in the space that has been occupied, then constructed and symbolized, by the populations they study. It is a fact that all societies—this is what defines them as such—have symbolized, marked, normed the space they mean to occupy, just as they have symbolized time, taken note of the regularities of the calendar, the cyclical return of the seasons, and tried to master intellectually the unknown factors and risks of weather. As we have said, this symbolizing activity confirms what Lévi-Strauss identified as man's urgent need for meaning, which, while it precedes the means of knowing, is not in its principle antagonistic to those means. From a more concretely historical perspective we should note that symbolization, namely, the symbolizing of space, is the *means* to unity, not necessarily its expression. Much ethnological research, in Africa, for example, shows how regions were populated in a relatively composite way; they have only gradually come to appear each as a place exclusive to a particular ethnic group. Such exclusivity is in some cases the result of a systematic political undertaking; in others it is the fruit of an illusion imposed from without, namely, by foreign colonizers.

Social groups symbolize space at different scales: for example, the interior of the house as well as groups of houses. The meaning created is expressed in residency rules, in divisions of the village into neighborhoods and sacred and profane zones. Agricultural land is distinguished from national territory, and the border is drawn between acculturated space and wilderness. Such symbolizing constructs relative identity by opposition to external otherness and as a function of internal otherness.

Using the term "segmentary logic," Evans-Pritchard in his renowned study of the Nuer brought to the fore the system of relative solidarities and oppositions that determine both social organization and the distribution of space. In the context he studied, lineage-based organization did in fact structure territorial organization, owing to the presence within each territorial segment of one of the dominant aristocratic lineages. This fact gave rise to a play of solidarities and conflicts: two groups related at the highest genealogical level might oppose each other, but they remained united against a group related to them only at a more distant genealogical level. Evans-Pritchard evoked the "structural relativity" of such groups, and without discussing in detail here the debates the notion of segmentary society has given rise to, let us keep in mind that at the level at which group identity through filiation is postulated, that identity is affirmed in relation to relative and external otherness on the one hand—other filiation-based groups—and internal otherness on the other, as defined in terms of sex, age, and status.

Anthropology has traditionally linked the question of otherness (or identity) to that of space, precisely because the symbolizing process carried out by social groups itself signifies that they set out to understand and master space so as to understand and organize *themselves*. This connection is not only expressed at the political level of territory or village but affects domestic life itself. It is remarkable that in societies geographically and historically quite distant from each other we find evidence of a shared felt need to set up lesser spaces and openings to the exterior, a need to symbolize home and threshold that is simultaneously the necessity to think or conceive identity and relation, same and other. Center, threshold, bor-

der are spatial notions applicable at the scale of domestic space. One
may evoke in this connection the couple Hestia-Hermes, whose
function in the classical Greek home has been analyzed by the anthropological historian Jean-Pierre Vernant,[15] as well as a divinity
such as Legba (or Echu) in the Ewe, Fon, or Yoruba regions of Western Africa and its various, more or less syncretic avatars in Haiti and
Brazil. Pantheon figures are doubly symbolic: they enable the conceiving of connection between interior and exterior in spatial terms,
and between same and other in psychological, sociological, and–
let's risk the word–ontological terms.

Indeed, the otherness that ritual systems take charge of and deal
with is *multiple* otherness. There is, as we know, the absolute otherness of the foreigner, the stranger-beyond-the-border on whom
one projects, as the need arises, all the defects whose presence is denied *chez soi*: ferocity, cannibalism, nonhumanity. And it is from
these absolutely external regions that events may suddenly spring
up: war, or the violence that is often at the origin of new political
formulas or arrangements. These events entail a recomposition of
space. Then there is internal otherness, social otherness, which is
in fact consubstantial with the social defined as a system of instituted differences. Gender, filiation, position in the sequence of siblings, age, are so many differential criteria that make up the social
weave, and they are not without spatial expression. Residency rules,
marriage prescriptions or interdictions, work obligations, are rigorously conceived, and they correspond to an extremely codified use
of space, for space is never used or frequented in free and undifferentiated ways.

It should be pointed out that this encoding of space is in no way
exclusive to sedentary societies. Nomads' journeys are placed under
the sign of repetition and involve identifying and remembering spatial details. The nomad encampment itself is never arbitrarily posi-
tioned: nomad habitations (tents, in the case of the Tuaregs) are
transmitted and inherited, and the principles of residence cannot be
transgressed. It is quite naturally in terms of internal social otherness that rules for using space are expressed; my example here is
taken from Dominique Casajus's study of the Kel Ferwan Tuaregs,
La Tente dans la solitude. The tent belongs to the wife. Whatever the
particular modes by which a tent is acquired (the oldest daughter is

privileged in this respect), every daughter ultimately possesses a tent of which her mother has woven at least a few panels. "In his wife's tent," writes Casajus, "a man is no better than a guest, whereas a woman can consider herself at home in her mother's tent as well as in her own."[16]

Finally, there is the otherness that I would propose to call inward otherness because it lodges in the person of every individual. As we noted in Chapter 1, all literature devoted to the notion of person shows that the individual has very often—and in extremely different cultures—been conceived as the ephemeral coming together, in a union lasting no longer than a lifetime, of principles or elements of various origins, certain of which are transmitted and inherited along socially recognized lines. It would be inexact to apply the term metempsychosis to all the beliefs about how an individual returns in the person of another; throughout Africa, for instance, it is a substance or a kind of authority that is believed to return. As we have said, the individual is by definition composite: relation is at the core of identity. Otherness and identity are inconceivable one without the other, not only in the social systems we have just evoked but in the instituted definition of the individual that is part of those systems. Consultations made at an individual's birth, or divination procedures that take the individual for object, are eminently social, and we discover this same ambivalence in the symbolic devices mentioned briefly here and in Chapter 1. They refer both to the connection between interior and exterior and to that between identity and relation, the individual and his or her entourage. Among the Ewe or the Fon, everyone has his or her *legba*, which, as we know, stands in the bedroom like a double of the person it protects from his or her own drives. But it is the same god Legba, this time singularized as a personage of the pantheon by myths, songs, and narratives, that is installed at the entrance to the house to keep others out, in the public square to protect exchanges, and at intersections— meeting places par excellence. And in this Legba is not unlike Hermes, another god of thresholds, borders, and exchanges, the god charged with leading each soul to its last resting place.

Three remarks will complete this brief evocation of symbolizing practices. The name attributed to each individual generally conveys both what that individual derives from others and his or her part of individual identity. The second of these, the individual's most individual part, elusive, fleeting, is generally symbolized in ritual activity as an ultimate but necessary unthinkable. Sometimes it is represented as a destiny (brought to light by divination at the moment of birth in the form of a sign, but a sign that, as we know, may be reinterpreted at every succeeding event), sometimes as a residue (a fistful of sand scooped up from the ground where the Fon diviner threw cowries or nuts during the birth consultation, then scattered at the moment of the individual's death). Finally, the individual body itself can be a space. While it may happen that the village space is conceived on the model of the human body, the opposite is still more frequent: the human body is conceived as an inhabited space where the relations of identity and otherness are incessantly played out. We know, for example, that in the gulf regions of Benin, an individual used to worship several parts of the body, believed to be the dwelling places of various principles and ancestral presences. From body to territory, from territory to body, a whole conception of anthropological place is affirmed, where the touchstones or landmarks of identity, relation, and history strive to settle into place.

One recognizes oneself in such a place. It is the oriented, "reconnoitered," symbolized center of the universes of recognition I evoked in the preceding chapter, universes from which all knowledge proceeds—universes that are therefore not in themselves, by themselves, objects of knowledge. Those who inhabit them, however, know them in detail (ethnographers have long remarked upon the excellent knowledge local specialists have of their natural milieu, or rather the painstaking attention and keen sense of observation that are reflected in the taxonomies they used and transmitted). In relations between people, recognizing oneself and where one is also means speaking the same language, and understanding one another with few words, following easily one's interlocutor's reasons—knowing the passwords.

It is here that the notion of non-place can help us characterize the situation I propose to call supermodernity. Supermodernity happens when history becomes current events, space becomes images, and the individual merely a gaze. In contrast to postmodernity, conceived of as an arbitrary sum of aleatory traits, supermodernity involves excess: three types of excess.

Excess time, first of all, or rather an excess of simultaneous events. If it seems to us that history has no meaning, this is because it is speeding up, coming closer. The minute our own individual past has been lived, it is inscribed in history. Events such as those we live each day have something to do with this feeling, but so does our vision of the immediate past; the role of news and the media in this vision cannot be denied. In the overabundance of media-covered facts that have to do with both our history and that of others (the "fifties," "sixties," "seventies," "eighties";[17] Vietnam, May 1968, the Berlin Wall, the Gulf War . . .), it is all the more difficult to find a main or guiding theme in that it is the meaning of our individual lives that is being called into question all at once. We've got history on our heels.

Next, excess space. This particular feeling of excess has to do with what must paradoxically be called the shrinking of the planet. The media project us instantaneously to the ends of the earth, and we feel affected by what's happening on the other side of the world from us at the very moment it happens. We can cite in this connection the televised reporting of the Gulf War (entirely symptomatic, more-over, of today's present-tense history, capable of making us feel that history has caught up with us) but also, even more immediately, the profusion of images in news or fiction in the midst of which we live as if such images were, in the end, hardly distinct from each other. At another level of representation, that figured by satellites turning incessantly in space, all territorial conflicts may look absurd, and threats to the environment, for instance, may seem indistinctly to concern the earth in its entirety.

Finally, excess individualism. In our media-covered world, every individual is directly called upon to testify. Each of us is the exclusive object of the man or woman who addresses us from the television screen. The acceleration of history and the shrinking of the planet are not without effect, as we know, on the relation an individual may have with him- or herself. Aggravating the precarious-ness of collective touchstones, they provoke what could be called a tendency to individualize purposeful action. Much of social behav-ior these days seems to wear the label chefs sometimes attribute to a dish that is in fact quite ordinary: *à ma façon* (prepared my way). I believe "my way"; I vote "my way"; I diet "my way." The point here

is not to analyze the illusion to which those who think they are acting "their way" may have fallen victim, but to underline the in-
creased importance of "the individual" in our behavior as well as
our representations. Advertising and the image of the body there
disseminated move in this direction, but so, in quite another area
and tone, does the language of human rights, which strips of all
credibility in advance anyone who invokes the alibi of culture or collective values to justify encroachments on individual freedom.

These three types of excess, it seems to me, have exercised and
continue to exercise an effective fascination on those who would
seem to be preserved from them by an institutional system. I am referring to people who are part of countries that, for political or religious reasons, are still far from being able to call themselves
"modern"; that is, open to differences and the consequences of difference. These are countries whose most progressive rallying cry is
in its essence contradictory: "How can we evolve without changing?"; or a variation of the same: "How is it possible to change this
part here but not that part there?" The rallying slogans of supermodernity–convergence of histories, deterritorialization of space,
liberation of the individual–are a fortiori foreign to them. Nonetheless, these words circulate among them and may be heard even
where they are not pronounced. They serve in mobilizing crowds
whose only language is that of nationalism–their first recourse–but
who also know that there is no freedom without individuals.

We see that the varieties of what I have been calling supermodernity form a paradox and a contradiction. In one sense, they open
each individual up to the presence of others; they correspond to the
ever-easier circulation of beings, things, and images. But in another
sense, they fold the individual back on himself, close her off, constituting him or her as a witness of rather than an actor in contemporary life. This contradiction is exemplarily expressed in the spaces
I have called non-places.

In non-places the three figures of supermodernity are particularly
legible. History is reduced to information: in gas stations the radio
stays on without interruption; newspapers are distributed in air-
planes; screens in airport waiting areas display the list of all flights
for a given day; my bank balance appears on the screen of the auto-
matic teller machine. The shrinking of space is particularly obvious

in airports, but can also be apprehended in department stores and supermarkets, where products from all over the earth are available, or in the image of credit cards "valid everywhere." Finally, the user of non-places, reduced to his function of passenger, consumer, or user, experiences a particular kind of solitude. Defined by his destination, the sum of his purchases, or his credit balance, the user of non-places "rubs shoulders" with millions of other individuals yet is alone: texts interpose themselves between him and the external world. The paradox of supermodernity culminates in non-places, where one is neither *chez soi* nor *chez les autres*.

A few qualifications are necessary here. First, notions of place and non-place obviously include notions of limit. There is non-place in every place, and in all non-places places can be recomposed. To put it another way, places and non-places, while they correspond to physical spaces, are also a reflection of attitudes, positions, the relations individuals have with the spaces they live in or move through. From this point of view, tourist travel is constitutive of non-places. The traveler is only passing from one place to another; this multiplicity is to be found later in the photos, slides, or lengths of film shown to friends once he or she has returned, in the narrative offered to them of his or her particular trip. We might be tempted to think that guidebooks (which are never read by the inhabitants of the places visited) compensate somehow for how quickly the traveler passes through and provide their users with otherwise missing information. But guidebooks are hardly ever read at home. Between the information delivered by guides or tourist brochures and the few instant images the traveler is able to record in the course of his or her itinerary; between the continuity of the documentary text and the anecdotal discontinuities of the trip (to say nothing of the narrative whose object it will become) we come upon the gaping emptiness of non-place. Non-place is the others' space without the others in it, space constituted in spectacle, a spectacle itself already hemmed in by the words and stereotypes that comment upon it in advance in the conventional language of folklore, the picturesque, or erudition.

The tourist trip is only used here as an example—nonetheless a particularly relevant one in that it combines movement and gaze-of what is tending to become our relation to others in the contemporary world. It is an abstract relation to the extent that it involves making the other into spectacle–in the strict sense, as when we exclaim over polished and illuminated monuments or fleetingly appreciate perspectives that can be discovered from the tiny airplane window or at a detour off the freeway. Or again, it could be in the sense of media spectacle, which we see in all television, radio, press, and advertising messages and images, messages and images that give us the feeling of being as close to the great of this world as to the damned of the earth precisely because we are connected to them only by words and images that we can neither use nor control. It is in all cases a distancing spectacle because of the optional or impossible character of dialogue and encounter: loudspeakers, answering machines, recorded messages, keyboards and screens seem to make the reciprocal exchange of words superfluous. The interchanges which have taken the place of intersections in freeway systems no doubt prevent automobile accidents, but they may stand as the very symbol of a space from which all possibility of encounter has been excluded.

Our sense of non-place also arises from a broad range of contemporary phenomena to which a significant part of humanity is subject and which wear no prestigious halo of free individual initiative. Next to traveling, there are all the moves imposed by global demography and the global economy: migrations that condemn migrants to make new places for themselves in spaces that are tending to close up, spaces they are not made to feel welcome in; massive urbanization as the response to the arrival of foreigners from within and without; camps where people from all over the earth who have been forced to clear out are settled for a time, all those who, like the Kurds and Palestinians, cannot find their place amid the official borders of world diplomacy and all those who, massed at borders in refugee camps, wait for the possibility of reinscribing themselves in the land of their origin, a possibility they hope will be made real by the return of peace and democracy. Refugee camps, transit camps, housing developments originally conceived to promote a workers' world but which have imperceptibly become the residual space in which homeless and unemployed people of various origins find themselves: all over the earth, spaces that cannot be qualified in terms of place, receive–temporarily, it is assumed–those whom the need to find employment or the realities of unemployment, poverty, war, or intolerance have forced to expatriate themselves, to undergo the poor man's urbanization, isolation, and confinement. The situations I have just too rapidly evoked are of course not equally hard or painful; let's say that some of them are worse than others. But they all have one point in common: they correspond to the loss of the social tie that is "normally" inscribed in place.

The era of workers' neighborhoods, when living quarters were near the factory, is over. In the huge housing projects on the periphery of French urban centers, the various elements of the population–blue-collar workers, white-collar workers, unemployed people, welfare recipients whether French or foreign–can only affirm their relative identity, which they measure against the ideal of the *petite bourgeoisie*, by marking themselves off from those whose proximity distances them both objectively and subjectively from that ideal. The work of Gérard Althabe and his research group is quite revealing in this regard. The vast systems of international charity and medical assistance that France has progressively championed force into the field of vision of the "haves," or at least of settled people, an image, every day more clearly perceived as "natural," of a humanity "beyond the pale," a humanity of tents and camps, food rations, plastic containers for fetching water. The important thing is not whether or not places are recomposed in these non-places, whether solidarities and sociability are recreated–of course they are. This is the price of survival. But in addition to the fact that they are minimal forms of localization–we might call it emergency localization, like emergency first aid–we must keep in mind that, in this context more than elsewhere, what is temporary is lived as if it were definitive. In the Western view, fed as it is by the media, the notions of "immigrant" (legal as well as illegal), "refugee," "camp" are becoming as taken for granted as those of our still recent taxonomies: "urban" and "rural," "sedentary" and "nomadic." At a time when nomads are being sedentarized and rural people transformed into emigrants-to-the-outskirts-of-town, it is the category of place that drops out of the picture. Its absence makes it harder to think about and conceive the other.

The other in his place, the other of postcards and tourist trips, the other dear to Mr. Le Pen–the one who stays at home, assuring us thereby, to use a time-honored French proverb, that *les vaches seront bien gardées*[18]–that other still exists, but he's on the move, diversifying, multiplying. He can't be assigned to a specific place, and I am not sure that in the eyes of those who cling to the ideal of having "their" land and "their" village, as if the meaning of their individual lives necessarily required them, the example of successful immigration is not more terrifying than that of illegal immigration. That one can leave home and remake a place for oneself elsewhere attests, in the eyes of the French at least, to the intellectual scandal of their own incapacity in years gone by to create genuine peopled colonies. What's frightening in the immigrant is the fact that he is also an emigrant.

It is thus not surprising that in the end we have difficulty conceiving space and otherness. The space problem is readily understood. We are experiencing a period in which great economic spaces are being created, large political spaces outlined, where multinational companies and capital "trespass" borders with a light and bounding step that can only make Marxists nostalgic, and where, simultaneously, empires are collapsing, nationalisms are being exacerbated, and, at a smaller scale, local museums are multiplying, together with references to miniscule local identities and demands to be able to work in one's own bit of country. The expression "identity crisis" is sometimes used in this connection, but what we are really looking at is a crisis of space–how is it possible to think simultaneously of the planet as a canton and my canton as a world?–and a crisis of otherness. It was the other's stability that made identity conceivable and easy. In the case of the remote other, this is obvious: one only saw him on condition of changing places oneself–going at least as far as the Exposition Coloniale. As for the internal other, more or less subtle categories have long been operative, divisions particular to class society and snobberies capable of marking all the nuances of what Pierre Bourdieu has called "distinction."

Today the category of the other has become blurred. But this is not to say that chauvinism, racism, and the spirit of class membership have disappeared. We might even suggest that, quite the contrary, because of the scrambling of signs, these attitudes could now become particularly intense. Failing to conceive the other, we construct the stranger.

Conclusion:
A Changed World, a Changed Object

I will, I hope, be pardoned for coming back at the end to my personal itinerary. It might be thought, because I use the word "itinerary" and because my latest published work was devoted primarily to an analysis of European facts and spaces, that I intend to relate or try to justify an itinerary in the shape of a round trip. Such a move is possible, whether one qualifies it as a return or, with the anthropologist and sociologist Georges Balandier, a detour. And it would seem fairly well adapted to the situation of an ethnologist who, growing older, is losing his taste for traveling and the global changes of a period whose accelerated developments tinge the traditional objects of classic ethnology with nostalgia or archaism. It would seem that the time has come for turning inward, that it is time for the ethnologist to turn ethnological eyes on self and the realities specific to this most modern world.

This is not, however, what I have chosen to do. I continue to return to Africa. The short essays I've written on certain aspects of French space and daily life have come between two books on African realities: *Le Dieu objet*, on the religions of Togo, and *N'Kpiti. La rancune et le prophète*, about an Ivorian prophet-healer.[1] Fundamentally, it seems to me, I have always tried, while working in a variety of areas and focusing on diverse empirical objects, to deepen exploration of the ultimate object of anthropological research–

the procedures by which meaning is constructed as they operate in various societies, procedures that depend on both individual initiatives and collective symbolic systems.

I would like, then, to suggest that the study I have conducted, first in Ivory Coast, then in Togo, of the systems of representation that local specialists make use of in interpreting events–events that touch individuals; more particularly, unhappy events–is not in itself different from the approach by which one may try to apprehend the procedures through which meaning is constituted in the most modern of societies. I am referring, of course, to social meaning, which always involves notions of identity and relation. The two approaches are that much less different in that the lineage-based world and the industrial world (to designate them summarily) now move together, and as far as their respective symbolic coherences are concerned, they are undergoing the same crisis. This is due to the fact that the diverse parts of humanity have now come into relation with each other (colonialism is only one form of this coming into relation, though no doubt the most aggressive and destructuring). It is also due, correlatively, to a process whereby consciousness is being individualized (or, if one prefers, individual solitude is being deepened). It is a crisis attested to by the recourse made just about everywhere in the world to new forms of religion, or, in another context, by the weakening of those intermediary rhetorics and "intermediary groups" such as trade unions that Durkheim saw as the surest means of insuring integration in the modern world. In this sense, the lineage-based world and the industrial world are not only contemporaneous, they belong to the same modernity.

In the lineage-based societies of Ivory Coast where I worked from 1965 to 1970 and to which I have never ceased returning, I was confronted with two types of reality, distinct and yet not really dissociable: systems of representation still operative in village societies, to which individuals referred in their attempts to interpret their daily lives; and a particular and internally diverse type of institution, prophetism, which arose at the beginning of the twentieth century. Africa in general, colonial Africa, was a land of prophets, prophet healers, who combined, in varying proportions, elements borrowed from lineage logics with the Christian message. This was how they worked to provide an effective answer to the anxieties, misfortunes,

illnesses, and incertitudes of those who came to them for help. In
Ivory Coast, as I mentioned in Chapter 5, the most celebrated of
these prophet healers was Harris, who was active throughout the region in 1913-14; most of the many prophets making themselves
heard today still claim him as their inspiration. Without entirely renouncing the old systems of interpretation, the prophets work to account for both misfortunes and troubles of the old variety (jealousy,
illness, death) and those that are not accounted for by classical grids
of interpretation, the new troubles: the city, unemployment, poor
school performance, professional failure.

In *Théorie des pouvoirs et idéologie*,[2] where I undertook a com-
parative analysis of lagoon societies in Ivory Coast, I put forward the
notion of "ideo-logic" as a way of defining the sum of the possible
and the thinkable within a single society. By this I mean the logic
underlying representations of nature and man, the body and its hu-
mors, transmission and influence; these include representations of
filiation and alliance and social rules in general. Ideo-logic differs
from cosmology conceived as a complete sum of representations of
the world and society in that it has to do with practice. It is a grammar in the form of instructions for use, a grammar in which the very
laying down of the rules of syntax identifies in every situation who
has the right to use that syntax. This is because not everyone has the
same right to speak—the right to use the same words or the same
right to use words—nor the same ability to master the system, even
when, from different points of view, everyone refers to the same ensemble of representations.

African prophetism shakes up lineage-based ideo-logic because it
proposes interpretive grids for events affecting people who are outside the framework of a given society or ethnic group and, comple-
mentarily, gives individuals more opportunity to speak.

Because it corresponds to syntagmatic orderings, the concept of
ideo-logic enabled me to render intellectually continuous notions
and realities which are ordinarily associated with distinct institutional domains. In short, it allows such notions and realities to remain as continuous with one another in the analysis as they are in
the discourses and practices of which they were both the constitutive element and the object.

Everyone combines in his or her own way the different symbolic systems Lévi-Strauss discusses in his *Introduction to the Work of Marcel Mauss*, using procedures of which the witchcraft trial scenarios I studied in *Théories des pouvoirs et idéologie* provide fully demonstrative examples. It is for economic sorts of reasons–the allotting of a harvest or a fishing haul–that two social partners, a maternal uncle and a uterine nephew, for example, call their relationship into question, one of them interpreting the physical troubles assailing him as a sign, as evidence, that an attack is being perpetrated on him by the other, then turning to paternal relatives or comrades in the same age group for support, asking them to call in a therapeutic-religious authority to defend him and bring him some relief. From this point of view, witchcraft scenarios are like all social scenarios that put people into relation with each other by bringing into relation swaths of reality–economic, religious, political, familial–that the language of institutions distinguishes and separates from one another.

Taking utterances and practices as objects of analysis can open up a perspective in which institutionalized distinctions are no longer at the fore. And from this perspective, it seems to me, we can reformulate the question of the relation between cultural and social, on the one hand, and individual and social (or collective) on the other. As both the logic of practices and the logic of representations, the sum total of the possible and the thinkable, ideo-logic cannot be reduced to the cultural, if by "cultural" we mean the social as the *represented* social–which seems to be how the concept of culture has most often been used in anthropological tradition. A certain number of symbolic representations concern the raw material of corporal identity and relation: birth, sexuality, reproduction, heredity, illness, or death. They have that raw material in common, within and despite the "diversity" of cultures and regardless of the form it may take in any given culture.

From this, two research directions came to seem possible. One was to analyze the forms and modes of power; the other, to analyze the individual's relations to the symbolic forms that give meaning to his or her doings and development. Designating a place that anthropologists have in no way finished exploring and that I was myself to visit in the following years (I am thinking particularly of my analyses in *Pouvoirs de vie, pouvoirs de mort*; *Génie du paganisme*;[3]

and *Le Dieu objet*), I remarked as early as *Théorie des pouvoirs et idéologie* that power always presents itself as the limit, and even the unthinkable aspect, of the social. Situated beyond the system of differences that organize and order the social, beyond the borders and the interdictions of which it is quite literally constituted, on the far side of transgression or of a break in continuity, power is the exception that founds the norm. Figures of power and domination—and, symmetrically, those of obedience, passive conformity, and subservience—are not, for all that, a matter of unconscious logic. We have seen how, in inversion rituals, either political or sexual, the dominated categories cry out the truth of social relations and domination, not so much inverting power relations as magnifying and caricaturing the manifestation of those relations. Figures of inversion (which I have suggested be labeled for this reason "inversion-perversion") are neither the cynical and alienating instrument with which power would make all serve its own purposes nor a pure form of subversion. They are both party to and constitutive of a more global ideo-logic; at one and the same time they assail and protect the space of power, ever threatened by history. Figures of prophetism are similar in this respect, and it was quite remarkable to observe in the 1960s that the discourse and practice of the best-known practicing prophet of Ivory Coast, Albert Atcho, could appear, depending on the moment and the analytic angle chosen, either as a model of alienation through acceptance of the existing order or as an expression of radical contestation, denunciation, or rejection.

Today, as prophetic movements multiply—this is itself a sign of subversion—the prophets' declarations of allegiance to the power in place, their openly affirmed will to encourage enterprising workers and stimulate development, are inseparable from the statements made by them about deficiency and inadequacy, statements that in turn relativize the scope and modify the meaning of such declarations and affirmations. Indeed, the prophet's word wouldn't mean anything if it were not first and foremost a response to "ill-being": misfortune, extreme poverty, illness. However conventional their remarks and interpretations may be, the prophets, by their mere existence, are situated precisely where ideo-logic offers a foothold to history, to reformulations and recompositions. Their ambiguity is in the image of the situation they are trying to understand and within which they seek to inscribe their presence and action. And the powers in place, fully aware of this, are careful to confine them to strictly therapeutic and religious activity, ready to intervene as soon as the prophets seem to be calling this house arrest into question or challenging the establishment.

My analysis of the individual life trajectories of some of the prophets' patients developed on two levels. What I observed in Africa induced me to formulate the notion of "therapeutic itinerary," which applies first of all to the experience of African patients who alternately look to healers and prophets for help, then to the hospital and practitioners of biological medicine (these last often at a loss to respond to them), then back to a prophet. Such itineraries are exemplary for at least two reasons. First, they correspond to a quest for meaning at the individual level at which putting the body to rights is not distinguished from restoring the social tie. Second, they correspond to a state of society in which it is no longer clear what the touchstones of identity and relation are.

These two considerations are perfectly applicable to modern industrial society, which is why I was led in some of my essays to evoke ordinary modes of constructing everyday meaning (see *La Traversée du Luxembourg*), then to reflect on the different types of spaces we regularly refer to today: the often mythic spaces of *terroir* (land, soil, heath) and *territoire* (see *Domaines et Châteaux*),[4] and the transportation and communication spaces of our age (airports, freeways, freeway interchanges, department stores, various networks of transmission and communication). In connection with this last type of space, one is tempted to imagine what could be termed, both paradoxically and contradictorily, an "ethnology of solitude." These spaces, which I have analyzed in *Non-Places*, correspond to a supermodernity characterized by the triple excess discussed in Chapter 6: excess event and image, which are linked to the media's influence in our lives, and excess individualization, which is a consequence of the weakening hold of collective cosmologies.

As I said in Chapter 6, the ethnological study of the proximal–of Europe, and specifically France–only acceded to the dignified status enjoyed by "exotic" ethnology, the study of the remote, by inscribing its analyses in space, thereby substituting the prosaic rigor of the monographic approach for the nostalgia and, in some cases, absence of control of the folkloristic one. Ethnology of the proximal appropriated what may be called "places of study," which constituted so many objects of analysis. But the particular contemporaneity with which anthropological analysis is confronted today is *not* essentially composed of places.

The fact that there are now non-places all over the earth (albeit in still unequal proportions), the simultaneous weakening of intermediary cosmologies or rhetorics that are based on the continuity and symbolization of place, and the ensuing dissolution of the social ties corresponding to those places–in sum, a certain solitary relation to the world–these are the facts of contemporary modernity. But this "delocalization" of the social was foreshadowed by a number of the phenomena studied by classical ethnology, specifically phenomena of what is called "cultural contact."

We have always tended to study such phenomena in connection with the urgencies of the particular moments in which they appear, and to study them by comparing them to past models that they are seen to modify and adapt. This is what Marshall Sahlins does in *Islands of History*,[5] when he notes that by placing their concepts and categories "in conspicuous relation to the world," Hawaiian societies exposed themselves to "functional reevaluation." Terminology, and in some cases institutions, remain, but their meaning changes. The notion of taboo, for example, which once designated the specific quality of things "reserved for the divinity," became, as a result of the ordeal of European contact, the simple sign of a right to own material property.

This analytic procedure is unquestionably legitimate, but the moment has perhaps arrived to consider contact phenomena, including its most spectacular forms–prophetism, messianism–from another point of view; that is, to consider them no longer simply modifications of the past and adaptations to a particular situation but as an anticipation of what has today become our common lot, our present contemporaneity. Colonized societies were the first to undergo the shock of globalization which is today reaching its term. The utopias they imagine and try to construct are in this respect revealing: clearly, the prophets are working to reconstruct places, cosmologies, and a language–a way of speaking. But in their efforts to keep their not particularly loyal patients and followers close to them–patients and followers pressed to find a remedy for their troubles, who rush from one healer to the next in between visits to the hospital or public clinic—the prophets end up underlining the singular, individual, and solitary character of these therapeutic and religious itineraries. And the ethnologist who studies this or that medical-religious institution is thus led, not to limit his or her observation to the community of which the healer or prophet dreams, but to take into consideration the multiplicity of individual trajectories that converge there more or less durably or ephemerally.

It might seem that, since Durkheim, the place of the individual in socio-anthropological research has been defined negatively: "There is no reason for the sciences of society to know the individual." To consider social facts as things is to admit that there is a level of observation and analysis at which we can and should leave individual intentions and particularities out of the picture. The highest ambitions of the social sciences have been inscribed in this current of thinking, which was perhaps most fully realized in the sum of thought and theory sometimes abusively unified under the term "structuralism."

But several aspects and stages must be distinguished here. Durkheimian sociology was not unaware of the diversity of the social or the effective power of emotions. In *The Division of Labor in Society* (1893), Durkheim already deplored the weakening of the "intermediary bodies"—schools, unions—which had enabled individuals of foreign origin to become integrated into the French nation. In *The Elementary Forms of the Religious Life*, he insisted not only on the collective character of representations of the social, which constituted in his view the truth of religious feeling, but also on the role of memory and commemoration, which he saw as accounting for the particular character of ceremonies in which a group simultaneously recognizes and remembers itself. Religious experience always involves an intellectual and affective fusion where the individual loses himself or herself in the shared consciousness of a collective destiny—though the individual is as necessary to that experience as he or she is overtaken by it.

This difficulty—namely, the presence-absence of the individual in anthropological analysis—regularly reappears in anthropologists' thought as the symptom of an anxiety that can elicit no reassuring reply–or as a poorly elucidated question: Who are anthropologists talking about when they talk about the people they talk about? Mauss's way of addressing this question was both clumsy and revealing. Parallel to the notion of "total social fact," he in effect proposed the notion of "total man." Total man was man studied in all his dimensions–physical, physiological, social, and so on–but also, and above all, total man was the "average" person. The notion of average person corresponded not to a statistical approximation but to a model that, in a certain state of society or in certain classes of society, corresponded to a reality. What individualizes people, Mauss in substance told us, is the reflective consciousness that enables "evolved" individuals to distance themselves from themselves and constitute a rampart against waves of collective emotion. Mauss was rightfully interested in such phenomena as obligation, or prayer conceived of as an efficient cause by the one who prays; he was interested in all instinctive "responses"–to which, we should note, mass movements bear a strong resemblance. But this was at the cost of distinguishing between evolved people (those of the "higher castes of our civilizations," who, he told us, are not generally those a sociologist should study) and less evolved people; and at the cost of assimilating less evolved *societies* with the least evolved *social strata* of *modern* societies. Reflective consciousness, real individuality, privileges of evolution and class, were not, in Mauss's understanding, the anthropologist's proper object. The anthropologist's purpose was to study the "total" man–that is, "instinctive" man, the "average" man:

> The ordinary man is already duplicated and feels himself to be a soul; but he is not master of himself. The average man of our days–and this is true above all of women–and almost all the men of archaic or backward societies, is a "total" man: he is affected in all his being by the least of his perceptions or by the least mental shock. The study of this "totality" is crucial, in consequence, for everything which does not concern the elite of our modern societies.[6]

We see, then, that renouncing the study of man in his individual dimension involves a biased conception of the "average" person (a being who could just as well be called "cultural" because all his or her attitudes are "instinctive" responses which are also responses coded and symbolized by culture). The "average" man has a less de-

veloped reflective consciousness and is thereby incapable of original initiatives. An equally biased conception of "evolved" man is
also proposed, the man of the "higher castes" of modern society,
whom Mauss, with a certain naiveté, believed was preserved from
the instinctive emotional upsurges of the masses.

The irrelevance of the individual dimension in the apprehension
of social facts has been postulated by approaches as opposed to each
other as culturalism and structuralism. In the one, we are still working within the theory of the average man; in the other, the researcher is interested in phenomena such as myth transformation
or the logic of systems of matrimonial alliance that have been posi-
tioned in the ethnologist's scheme at another level than that of social practices.

It is not my purpose at this point to evoke theories that rely upon
the facts of interaction to show, on the contrary, that the social derives from individual behaviors. I mean rather to suggest that within
anthropological procedure, which by definition works to apprehend
comparable totalities, the individual is securing an ever more certain place for himself—or herself.

When we speak of meaning in anthropology we mean the meaning that people can give to their reciprocal relations with one another. Once again, we mean social meaning. And it is none other
than social meaning that individuals are talking about when they
worry about the meaning of their lives. For those in France and elsewhere who are (or were) members of political parties or unions,
those organizations did not metaphorically or secondarily give
meaning to life; rather, they prefigured what should be—what should
have been—satisfying social relations in which the identity of each
person could be fully experienced in the relation with others. We
know that this is not, or is not any longer, always the case; far from
it—and what we often hear people talking about today is indeed a crisis of meaning both in the domain of the individual (which includes
the couple and the family) and that of collective institutions (society, the state).

One element of the crisis seems to me to reside in the substitution of media for mediations, a substitution characteristic of our
modernity. The object of the media message (the "target," as ad-
vertisers put it) is the individual defined according to his or her

functions of consumer or citizen. Conversely, what is presented to our attention are texts and images that have to do with the world in its entirety. This observation is not meant to suggest that there is no possible sociology of the media or the social issues raised by the different types of media operating today, but rather to underline the fact that the procedures by which meaning is elaborated are now confided to individuals themselves, who are invited to think about them, to think something of them, for and by themselves. It is important, then, not to denounce the probable effects of illusion (such effects are of course inherent in all cosmologies) but to understand in its generality a particular variety of the human situation that we haven't quite encountered before and to study its manifestations.

These manifestations are to be found in at least two types of phenomena. We have already discussed the anonymous spaces of circulation, communication, broadcasting. But surely it is necessary to consider as equally characteristic of our modernity the phenomena traditionally studied by ethnologists under the approximative name of "syncretism." The religious forms that are proliferating now—prophetism, sects, various fundamentalisms—all have in common the fact that they are addressed to sick or unhappy individuals no longer able to situate themselves in relation to one another through old mediations or cosmologies, and who suffer in a way from a deficit of meaning.

We have reached the time of generalized anthropology, an anthropology without exoticism. In such anthropology the study of the social can no longer fail to take into account the ideological reality of the individual. A few lines by Michel Leiris will help us conclude on this point. In a short article published in 1930 entitled "L'homme et son intérieur," Leiris, discussing the human body, wrote:

> If we each had to remain alone, reduced to the image of our body set face to face with external nature, this position would be grand perhaps—that of a god or a hero—but more awful than any other, for we would never understand what that other thing is, so distinct from our being, so indifferent to us, so distantly, glacially foreign. What gives us the possibility of connecting ourselves to it is the existence of human creatures other than ourselves who serve the function of mediation thanks to the fact that they partake of nature (they are external, like nature) while also partaking of ourselves (because they are con-

stituted in almost the same way we are). So it is that society ends up being the tie between nature and ourselves, and our human relations immediately become the most important of the numerous relations that exist between ourselves and the world.[7]

We might complete this analysis by pointing out that the image of different societies, of "human creatures" who were *other* than ourselves in two ways—first, like all others, even those close to us, they were simply not ourselves; but second, they were also visibly culturally marked, stamped with a certain difference, and in this, they were exotic—added a supplementary dimension to this mediating function. Now, in the media age and with the death of exoticism, a kind of short-circuit is produced that confronts each individual directly with the image of the world. Difficulty in symbolizing relations between people is stimulating a multiplication and individualization of cosmologies. This phenomenon itself constitutes for the anthropologist an object of study that is multiple, fascinating, paradoxical, and new.

On the horizon of anthropological research we are now able to glimpse the possibility of an anthropology without exoticism. Beginning with Romanticism, exoticism, together with the sense of distance, has stood as simultaneous proof of relative resemblance and radical difference. An exotic religion was one that offered enough relevant traits for a Christian to be able to recognize it as a religion, while presenting that same Christian with postulates and rituals that were disturbing enough in his eyes to cause him to wonder about them and be tempted to see in them either an outline or a degenerated version of the true religion, or even to conclude that this was a kind of magic. Perhaps magic was nothing more, after all, than the others' religion. The same was the case when the distanced observer turned to matters of power, the family, economy *chez les autres*. The exotic reality he saw reminded him of the reality which was his own frame of reference; it reminded him of it enough that he was tempted to speak of it in the same terms he applied to his own. This is what we call ethnocentrism—the blatant ethnocentrism of, for example, the *coutumiers* written by French colonial officers or administrators, who tried to express in terms of French law the modes of social life or economic exchange particular to the African societies they considered themselves responsible for. But the arti-

fice of language only underlined the disturbing, discrepant quality
of a reality that will not submit to it. This led to the debates so familiar to us on the presence or absence in such societies of the
state–or of any political life at all; on the latent monotheism of poly-
theisms; on the relevance or irrelevance for analysis of notions such
as dowry, contract, exploitation. Whether it is accounted for in evolutionist, culturalist, diffusionist, or Marxist terms, the obvious fact
of this discrepancy was always what led us to think of ethnology as
the scientific study of *others*. Moreover, exoticism was not tied to ge-
ographic distance or even to ethnic belonging: ethnologists studying Europe at first took for objects surviving customs, traditions,
and human milieux (peasants, artisans) that were imbued for them
with a kind of internal exoticism.

Exoticism is disappearing today. It is disappearing because of the
generalized spatial and ideological effects I have associated with the
notion of supermodernity. But it is also disappearing because, in the
light of those effects, we realize that a good part of what ethnology
has been studying for long years as exotic realities–messianisms,
prophetisms, syncretisms, the sum of "contact" phenomena, and
more particularly those having to do with massive transfers of population linked to slavery–actually anticipated and corresponded to
an acceleration of history, a shrinking of space, and an individualization of consciousness that, prolonged and amplified, characterize fairly accurately our supermodernity. Conversely, the category
of syncretism is running in neutral today because we let it explain
anything, especially in highly industrialized countries. It is no
longer operative because it depended on an effect of distance whose
disappearance is precisely what characterizes contemporaneity. The
death of exoticism thus opens up a new field of exploration for anthropology, which is called upon now, perhaps more than ever before, to reflect on renewed categories of space and otherness.

Reference Matter

Notes

Chapter 1

1. A *coutumier* is a written inventory and description of the customs followed by the people of a given territory, region, or country. Here the author is referring more specifically to the *coutumiers* written by French colonial administrators about the ways of life among the indigenous populations–the colonized–of the country's African and Asian colonies.–Trans.

2. Marcel Mauss, *Sociologie et anthropologie*, preceded by Claude Lévi-Strauss's "Introduction à l'oeuvre de Marcel Mauss," 3rd ed. expanded (Paris: Presses Universitaires de France, 1966). Parts 3, 4, 5, and 6 of Mauss's text are available in English under the title *Sociology and Psychology*, trans. Ben Brewster (London: Routledge, 1979). Lévi-Strauss's brief text has been published separately as *Introduction to the Work of Marcel Mauss*, trans. Felicity Baker (London: Routledge & Kegan Paul, 1987). Subsequent page numbers in parentheses refer to this edition.

3. Cornelius Castoriadis, *L'Institution imaginaire de la société* (Paris: Editions du Seuil, 1975). Published in English as *The Imaginary Institution of Society*, trans. Kathleen Blamey (Cambridge: Polity Press, 1987).

4. Louis Althusser, *Pour Marx* (Paris: François Maspero, 1965; 2nd ed. Paris: Editions de la Découverte, 1986). Available in English as *For Marx*, trans. Ben Brewster (London: Penguin; New York: Pantheon, 1969).

5. Jacques Lacan, "L'Agressivité en psychanalyse," originally published in *Revue française de Psychanalyse* 3 (Jul.-Sept. 1948) and reprinted in *Ecrits* (Paris: Editions du Seuil, 1966), pp. 101-24. Published in English as "Aggressivity in Psychoanalysis" in *Ecrits: A Selection*, trans. Alan Sheridan (New York: Norton, 1977), pp. 8-29.

6. Castoriadis, *The Imaginary Institution of Society*, p. 117.

7. Romorantin is a village in the Loire valley–an example of a small town in the middle of nowhere.–Trans.

8. Castoriadis, p. 128.

9. Ibid., p. 163.

10. Samir Amin, *Le Développement du capitalisme en Côte-d'Ivoire* (Paris: Editions de Minuit, 1967).

11. In the wars between rival groups of Amazonian Tupinamba (whose cannibalism was evoked by Montaigne in the *Essais*), the fundamental rule was accepted by all: the vanquished were brought to live among their conquerors, there to take a wife and to await–without attempting to flee–the often distant day of their execution. See Hélène Clastres, "Les beaux-frères ennemis. A propos du cannibalisme tupinamba," *Nouvelle Revue de psychanalyse* 6 (1972): 71-84.

12. Paulin Hountondji, *Sur la "philosophie africaine"* (Paris: François Maspero, 1977).

13. The reference is to Montesquieu's *Lettres persanes* (1721), where the imagined correspondence of a Persian visitor to Paris is used to satirize the French themselves and their institutions.–Trans.

14. Claude Lévi-Strauss, *Introduction to the Work of Marcel Mauss*, p. 26.

15. Ibid., pp. 30-31.

16. Ibid., pp. 27-28.

Chapter 2

1. The reference here is to Pierre Corneille's play *Les Horaces*. Based on an account by Livy, the play tells the story of the relations between two rival families, the Horaces of Rome and the Curiaces of the ancient city of Alba Longa. The conflict between filiation and alliance that moves the story forward is particularly bloody: a sister of the three Horace brothers is betrothed to one of the three Curiace brothers; one of her brothers concludes the battle that opposes the two sets of sons by killing all three of the Curiace brothers, including of course his sister's fiancé. When, after his triumphant return to Rome, his sister assails him for having killed the man she was to marry and whose family she already feels bound to, he kills his sister. (Until recently, *Les Horaces* fig-

ured with great regularity on reading lists for French ninth-graders, as familiar to the French as *Romeo and Juliet* to English speakers.)–Trans.

2. The expression could be translated roughly as "daily record." In their *carnets du jour* French newspapers publish birth, wedding, and death announcements paid for by the family or friends concerned.–Trans.

3. In *Le Dieu objet* (Paris: Flammarion, 1988) I undertook, starting from a rereading of the anthropologist Bernard Maupoil, a minute analysis of the incessant referring of same back to other which is observable in birth and death rites among the Fon of former Dahomey.

4. Stephen Hawking, *A Brief History of Time* (London: Bantam, 1988), p. 193.

5. The ethnological study of individuals and groups close to, rather than remote from, the anthropologist's own cultural and/or social origins; see Chap. 3.–Trans.

6. Claude Lévi-Strauss, *Structural Anthropology*, trans. C. Jacobson and B. G. Schoepf (New York: Basic Books, 1963), p. 21 (pp. 27-28 of the original, *Anthropologie structurale* [Paris: Plon, 1958]).

7. Bernard Maupoil, *La Géomancie à l'ancienne côte des Esclaves* (Paris: Institut d'ethnologie, 1943; 3rd ed. 1988); Pierre Verger, *Notes sur le culte des orisa et vodun à Bahia, la Baie de tous les saints, au Brésil et à l'ancienne côte des Esclaves en Afrique* (Dakar: Institut français d'Afrique noire, 1957) and *Orisha. Les dieux yoruba en Afrique et au Nouveau Monde* (Paris: Métailié, 1982).

Chapter 3

1. Marcel Mauss, *Oeuvres*, vol. 3 (Paris: Editions de Minuit, 1969), p. 359.

2. Ibid., p. 361 (review first published in *L'Année sociologique* 3, 1900).

3. Ibid., p. 369 (text first published in the *Revue de l'histoire des religions* 45, 1902).

4. Much French ethnological study of "self" has been done within the contexts or frameworks the author lists here–studies of relations between people living in the same housing project, for example, or of the ways that working for or in a given business corporation affect the lives and relations of all those who do.–Trans.

5. Claude Lévi-Strauss, *Race et Histoire* (Paris: Denoël, 1961). Published in English as *Race and History* (Paris: UNESCO, 1952, 1968).

6. Marcel Mauss, *Oeuvres*, vol. 3, p. 359.

7. The author defines rites of inversion and discusses them at some length in Chapter 4.–Trans.

8. Clifford Geertz, *The Interpretation of Cultures* (New York: Basic Books, 1973), p. 409.

9. Ibid., p. 408.

10. Ibid., p. 452, note 43.

11. The word *beur* is the French word *Arabe* pronounced "backward" (an example of a way of playing with language that is a little like pig-Latin and whose use is associated with French teenagers). More precisely, a *beur* is a young person born in France of parents who came there from the former North African colonies of which they were indigenous inhabitants. The author is alluding here to the French mass media's appropriation of what may be considered an "in-group" term.–Trans.

Chapter 4

1. This is a play on the French proverb *Chacun à sa place et les vaches seront bien gardées* ("Let each keep to his place and the cows will be well watched"–all will remain in prosaic good order).–Trans.

2. See Jean Froissart, *Voyage en Béarn*, prefaced by Marc Augé (Paris: Olivier Orban, 1987). [In English see Froissart, *Chronicles*, ed. Gillian and William Anderson (Carbondale: Southern Illinois Press, 1963).–Trans.]

3. The expression reflects the belief that a witch can be in two places at once, or rather that a certain element or agent can leave the witch's body and make things happen in another place. This element is something like that individual's "double."–Trans.

4. References are to Harry Kemelman's Rabbi Small and Tony Hillerman's Jim Chee.–Trans.

5. George Devereux, *Ethnopsychoanalysis: Psychoanalysis and Anthropology as Complementary Frames of Reference* (Berkeley: University of California Press, 1978), pp. 228-29.

6. Ibid., p. 242.

7. I treat the matter of inversion-perversion at length in *Pouvoirs de vie, pouvoirs de mort* (Paris: Flammarion, 1977).

8. Max Gluckman, "The Role of the Sex in Wiko Circumcision Ceremonies," in M. Fortes, ed., *Social Structure: Studies Presented to A. R. Radcliffe-Brown* (Oxford: Clarendon Press, 1949), pp. 145-67.

9. The reference is to the main character in Molière's *Bourgeois Gentilhomme*, who in a famous scene requests his tutor to help him find a more stylish version of the sentence "*Belle marquise, vos beaux yeux me font mourir d'amour*." The professor responds with four variations, each more syntactically scrambled than the last but none incomprehensible in itself, in part because crucial syntactic sequences–*belle marquise, vos beaux yeux*–are left intact.–Trans.

10. Norman Cohn, *The Pursuit of the Millenium: A History of Popular Religious and Social Movements in Europe from the Eleventh to the Sixteenth Century* (London: Secker and Warburg, 1957).

11. Victor Margueritte (1866-1962) was a French writer whose realist works regularly addressed the question of women's sexual emancipation. *La Garçonne* created a scandal and led to his being dropped from the order of the Legion of Honor.–Trans.

12. George Devereux, *Ethnopsychoanalysis*, p. 174.

Chapter 5

1. In France as in most of Europe–and in direct contrast to the United States–lower-income people tend to be pushed out of city centers by unaffordable rents toward outskirts and suburbs, where they often live in vast state-subsidized housing developments. It is to such developments that the author refers.–Trans.

2. Milan Kundera, *The Art of the Novel*, trans. from French by Linda Asher (New York: Grove Press, 1988), pp. 35-36.

3. Sigmund Freud, *The Future of an Illusion*, ed. James Strachey, The Penguin Freud Library, vol. 12 (Penguin, 1985), p. 240.

4. The first of these pejorative expressions refers to a cynical "politics for the sake of politics" manipulation of voters reflecting an absence of concern for the public interest, while the second–literally, "wooden tongue"–was originally used to characterize the speaking style of the Communist Party and designates ideologically rigid, stereotyped language, implying a refusal to answer questions directly and, more generally, to take account of events or changes in public opinion.–Trans.

5. The reference is to the former dictator of the Central African Republic, Jean-Bedel Bokassa. Beginning his career as a petty officer in the French army, Bokassa seized power in 1966 after France had granted independence to the region, then had himself crowned emperor–Napoleon-style–in 1976.–Trans.

6. The reference is once again to Molière's *Bourgeois Gentilhomme*: Monsieur Jourdain has "done" prose without knowing what it is.–Trans.

Chapter 6

1. See Isaac Chiva, "Entre livre et musée. Emergence d'une ethnologie de la France," in Chiva and Utz Jeggle, eds., *Ethnologies en miroir. La France et les pays de langue allemande* (Paris: Editions de la Maison des sciences de l'homme, 1987), pp. 9-33.

2. Robert Hertz, *Mélanges de sociologie religieuse et de folklore* (Paris: Alcan, 1928), pp. 131-94.

3. Louis Dumont, *La Tarasque. Essai de description d'un fait local d'un point de vue ethnographique* (Paris: Gallimard, 1951).

4. Christian Bromberger, "Du grand au petit. Variations des échelles et des objets d'analyse dans l'histoire récente de l'ethnologie de la France," in *Ethnologies en miroir* (pp. 67–94), p. 68.

5. The word *commune* designates the smallest French political and administrative territorial unit; there are about 18,000 *communes* in France. A *commune* can of course be a fairly large city, but the word often evokes a small town, sometimes as part of a large rural area.–Trans.

6. Albert Soboul, "Esquisse d'un plan de recherches pour une monographie de communauté rurale," *La Pensée* 13 (1947), pp. 34–50.

7. Lucien Bernot and René Blancard, *Nouville, un village français* (Paris: Institut d'ethnologie, 1953).

8. Laurence Wylie, *Village in the Vaucluse* (Cambridge, Mass: Harvard University Press, 1961).

9. Georges Ravis-Giordani, *Bergers corses. Les communautés villageoises du Niolu* (Aix-en-Provence: Edisud, 1983).

10. Agnès Fine, "Le parrain, son filleul et l'au-delà," *Etudes rurales* 105, 106 (1987), pp. 123–46.

11. Tina Jolas, "La part des hommes. Une société de chasse au bois," *Etudes rurales* 87–88 (1982), pp. 345–56; Claudine Fabre-Vassas, "Le partage du *ferum*. Un rite de chasse au sanglier," ibid., pp. 377–400.

12. Martine Segalen, introduction to *L'Autre et le Semblable. Regards sur les sociétés contemporaines* (Paris: Presses du CNRS [Centre national de recherches scientifiques], 1989), pp. 7–14.

13. Once again, in France and in Europe generally, poorer people tend to live outside city centers.–Trans.

14. See *Non-Places: Introduction to an Anthropology of Supermodernity* (originally published as *Non-lieux, Introduction à une anthropologie de la surmodernité*, Paris: Editions du Seuil, 1992), trans. John Howe (London: Verso, 1995).

15. Jean-Pierre Vernant, "Hestia-Hermès. Sur l'expression religieuse de l'espace et du mouvement chez les Grecs," chap. 3 of *Mythe et pensée chez les Grecs: études de psychologie historique* (Paris: Maspero, 1965). Translated into English under the title *Myth and Thought in Ancient Greece* (London: Routledge & Kegan Paul, 1983).

16. Dominique Casajus, *La Tente dans la solitude. La société et les morts chez les Touaregs Kel Ferwan* (Paris: Editions de la Maison des sciences de l'homme, 1987), p. 69.

17. The decade names are in English in the original.–Trans.

18. See Chap. 4, note 1.

Conclusion

1. Marc Augé, *Le Dieu objet* (Paris: Flammarion, 1988), and, with Jean-Paul Colleyn, *N'Kpiti: la rancune et le prophète* (Paris: Editions de l'Ecole des hautes études en sciences sociales, 1990).

2. Marc Augé, *Théorie des pouvoirs et idéologie: étude de cas en Côte-d'Ivoire* (Paris: Hermann, 1975).

3. Marc Augé, *Pouvoirs de vie, pouvoirs de mort: introduction à une anthropologie de la répression* (Paris: Flammarion, 1977), and *Génie du paganisme* (Paris: Gallimard, 1982).

4. Marc Augé, *La Traversée du Luxembourg, Paris, 20 juillet 1984: ethno-roman d'une journée française considérée sous l'angle des moeurs, de la théorie, et du bonheur* (Paris: Hachette, 1985), and *Domaines et Châteaux* (Paris: Editions du Seuil, 1989).

5. Marshall Sahlins, *Islands of History* (University of Chicago Press, 1965).

6. Marcel Mauss, *Sociology and Psychology* (London: Routledge, 1979), p. 28.

7. Michel Leiris, *Brisées* (Paris: Gallimard Folio, 1992), p. 59.

Complementary Sources

Chapter 1

On slavery in Africa, see Claude Meillassoux, ed., *L'Esclavage en Afrique précoloniale* (Paris: François Maspero, 1975), and Claude Meillassoux, *Anthropologie de l'esclavage* (Paris: Presses Universitaires de France, 1986).

On the notion of "person," see *La Notion de personne en Afrique Noire* (papers from an international colloquium held in 1971 organized by Germaine Dieterlen, Paris: Editions du CNRS, 1973).

On the the king's double body, see Ernst Kantorowicz, *The King's Two Bodies: a Study in Medieval Political Theology* (Princeton, N.J.: Princeton University Press, 1957).

On the notions of cosmology and *chez soi*, see Vincent Descombes, *Proust: philosophie du roman* (Paris: Editions de Minuit, 1987).

On symbolizing the difference between the sexes, see Françoise Héritier, "Le sang du guerrier et le sang des femmes. Notes anthropologiques sur le rapport des sexes," in *Cahiers du GRIF* (*Groupe de recherche et d'information féministe*) 29 (Winter 1984-85), pp. 7-21.

On the fetish, see Jean Bazin, "Corps de dieux," in *Le Temps de la réflexion* 7 (1986), pp. 253-73.

Chapter 2

On symbolism, belief, and the limits of ethnographic description, see Dan Sperber, *Rethinking Symbolism*, trans. Alice Morton (Cambridge: Cambridge University Press, 1975).

On conceptions of political power as deriving from a particular
strength, see Georges Balandier, *Political Anthropology*, trans. A. M.
Sheridan Smith (New York: Pantheon, 1970). See also Emmanuel
Terray, *La Politique dans la caverne* (Paris: Editions du Seuil, 1991).

Chapter 3

On the contrast between "hot" and "cold" historical contexts, see
Georges Charbonnier, *Entretiens avec Claude Lévi-Strauss* (Paris:
Julliard, 1991 [1961]).

On inversion rituals associated with interregnum periods and relations between the king's person and his "double," see the following
studies on the Agni: Henriette Diabaté, "Le Sannvin: un royaume
akan de la Côte-d'Ivoire (1701–1901)," doctoral thesis, Ecole des
hautes études en sciences sociales, 1984; and Claude-Hélène Perrot,
Les Anyi-Ndenye et le pouvoir aux 18ème et 19ème siècles (Paris:
Publications de la Sorbonne / Abidjan: Publications CEDA, 1982).

The "postmodernist" temptation in anthropology is clearly re-
vealed in James Clifford and George E. Marcus, eds., *Writing Culture:
The Poetics and Politics of Ethnography* (Berkeley: University of California Press, 1986).

See also Georges Balandier, *Le Désordre. Eloge du mouvement*
(Paris: Fayard, 1985).

Chapter 4

On the relations between the rational and the cultural, and more
specifically, on the necessity of interpreting misfortune, see Vincent
Descombes, *Philosophie par gros temps* (Paris: Editions de Minuit,
1989); and Jeanne Favret-Saada, *Les Mots, la mort, les sorts: la sorcel-
lerie dans le Bocage* (Paris: Gallimard Folio, 1985 [1977]).

On power relations / meaning relations, the essential reference remains Pierre Bourdieu, *Outline of a Theory of Practice*, trans. Richard
Nice (Cambridge: Cambridge University Press, 1977).

On cannibalism, see the *Nouvelle revue de psychanalyse* 3, "Destins
du cannibalisme" (1972), and on the divine king, see Claude Tardits's
entry in the *Encyclopaedia Universalis*, 1989 ed., s.v. "roi divin."

Chapter 5

It would be interesting to relate the notion of "universes of recogni-
tion" to the idea of "world" put forward by Luc Boltanski and Laurent
Thévenet in *De la justification: les economies de la grandeur* (Paris:
Gallimard, 1991).

On the relations between anthropology and illness, see Marc Augé and Claudine Herzlich, eds., *Le Sens du mal: anthropologie, histoire, sociologie de la maladie* (Paris: Editions des Archives contemporaines, 1984), and Didier Fassin, *Pouvoir et maladie en Afrique: anthropologie sociale dans la banlieue de Dakar* (Paris: Presses universitaires de France, 1992).

The reciprocal construction of the other by observer and observed is at the center of Gérard Althabe's work and is already clearly laid out in *Oppression et libération dans l'imaginaire: les communautés villageoises de la côte est de Madagascar* (Paris: Editions de la Découverte, 1982 [1969]).

Chapter 6

On the relations between a society and "its" nature, see Philippe Descola, *La Nature domestique: symbolisme et praxis dans l'écologie des Achouar* (Paris: Editions de la Maison des Sciences de l'Homme, 1986).

On anthropological study of French suburbs (*les banlieues*) and housing projects, see "Ethnologie urbaine," *Terrain* 3 (October 1984). See also Pierre Bourdieu, *La Misère du monde* (Paris: Editions du Seuil, 1993).

On the notion of "stranger" illustrated with African examples see W. A. Shack and E. P. Skinner, eds., *Strangers in African Societies* (Berkeley: University of California Press, 1979).

Finally, on the discovery and perception of the "other," see Tzvetan Todorov, *The Conquest of America: the Question of the Other*, trans. Richard Howard (New York: Harper and Row, 1984).

Library of Congress Cataloging-in-Publication Data

Augé, Marc

   [Sens des autres. English]

   A sense for the other : the timeliness and relevance of anthropology /
Marc Augé; translated by Amy Jacobs.

     p.   cm. – (Mestizo Spaces)

   Includes bibliographical references.

   ISBN 0-8047-3034-2 (cloth). – ISBN 0-8047-3035-0 (pbk.)

   I. Anthropology–Philosophy.   I. Title.   II. Series.

GN33.A8413   1998

301'.01–dc21   97-26448

                                                      CIP

∞   This book is printed on acid-free, recycled paper.

Original printing 1998

Last figure below indicates year of this printing:

07 06 05 04 03 02 01 00 99 98

A Sense for the Other

*The Timeliness
and Relevance of
Anthropology*

Mestizo Spaces
Espaces Métissés

V. Y. Mudimbe
EDITOR

Bogumil Jewsiewicki
ASSOCIATE EDITOR